Ornamental Grasses

Stefan Leppert

Ornamental Grasses

Wolfgang Oehme and the New American Garden

F

FRANCES LINCOLN LIMITED
PUBLISHERS

Contents

Introduction
A mysterious man in a mysterious land

In the autumn of 2006 I was witness to a wonderful conversation. It took place near Baltimore in Maryland, and was brief. Over seventy years old, a lightly-dressed, utterly soaked man came in from pottering around his garden in the pouring rain. His daughter-in-law, who had just moved in, was flabbergasted. 'Wolfgang, it's raining. You must put something else on or at least take an umbrella,' she said. 'Rain doesn't bother me. I'm a plant. Plants need rain,' came the reply, with a broad smile. His daughter-in-law, wrapped in a woolly sweater, just shivered. I was reminded of Karel Čapek, who managed to capture perfectly the essence of the gardener: 'Even when choked by grey fog and soaked by cold rain, the gardener is not bothered,' wrote the Czech in the 1930s. The flowers and plants are what matter.

A few days later I was having dinner with a lady and this waterproof man. After he'd filled himself up with a great heap of raw vegetables and boiled potatoes, without

Top left: Wolfgang Oehme in Charleston, South Carolina. The newly minted American was very interested in the history of the United States and the places it was written.

Left: The man in the sunbleached shirt, under a cap softened by a thousand and one rain showers and stiffened again by the heat, prefers whenever possible to live outdoors.

In the first few years after leaving Germany, Wolfgang Oehme's plane landed in New York. Now and then he took time to dive into the ocean of skyscrapers that was Manhattan. The Empire State Building was at this time the world's tallest.

having drunk so much as a drop, he drained his glass of water in one gulp. 'I'm a plant, I love earth, I love water, I drink water, I eat earth,' he declared. 'But Wolfgang,' the lady replied, 'you can't just live off earth.' 'You're right. Sometimes there's a bit of greenery with some roots hanging off it, dandelions or something.' We laughed. Had we understood him correctly, this mysterious man?

I'd visited Wolfgang Oehme once before, ten years earlier, to see his gardens for myself. It had long been accepted in Europe that he and his business partner, James van Sweden, had revolutionised garden design in the United States. I was driven to ask how this dramatic claim could be justified. What was it about their gardens that was so radical? Was Wolfgang Oehme really a flowerbed revolutionary? Certainly, there has been at least a small revolution in America's parks and gardens. When Oehme arrived in Baltimore in 1957 to begin his new life, he was confused and dismayed. There were no herbaceous perennials or ornamental grasses to be seen at all. Wherever he looked he saw, above all, one thing – lawns, on a huge scale, bordered by lone shrubs and trees, and so for the young man from an unassuming home in Saxony it wasn't just the American cars and the skyscrapers that seemed inconceivably enormous. Almost forty years after his arrival, as we drove through Maryland, Oehme was constantly waving his hands and pointing out plants, mostly high grasses or perennials, often just giving us their names. *Miscanthus* here,

Top: From his very first days in the United States the immense lawns of North American houses offended Oehme. He soon decided to transform these shaven wastes into luxuriant landscapes of perennials and ornamental grasses.

Opposite: Lushness, abundance and variety of colour characterise these two gardens in the hills of Pennsylvania and Virginia. Plants continue to flower until late autumn, and those that have faded enrich the scenery with attractive seedheads.

Calamagrostis there, *Eupatorium* on the right, *Senecio* to the left – none of this was here before he arrived. You could hear the pride in his voice.

The hand-waving, the scattering of mumbled sentences into the silence continues, and the plants that Wolfgang Oehme points out have multiplied. Lawns, shorter and denser than soft carpets in living rooms, still proliferate. Wolfgang Oehme is a peaceful, tolerant spirit, but his lifelong enemy, the lawn, remains. All those who live out their childhood dreams of being simple farmers on their mini tractors, all those who tame their once wild country with a good deal of engine noise – Oehme would most like to pull their ride-on mowers from under their backsides, if only he could.

Wolfgang Oehme knows what he can do: lay out wonderful gardens, create splendid plant pictures. But does he know what he is – beyond a mysterious man in a mysterious land? He's neither soldier nor missionary, has neither weapons nor a comprehensive vocabulary. Or perhaps, in his own way, he is both. His weapons are his plants, sometimes secretly planted, which provide an alternative to the evergreen garden desert. They are also his vocabulary, they encompass everything that moves his spirit as a gardener and say clearly what he can only laboriously express in words.

Possibly more than any other living garden designer, Wolfgang Oehme's life and work are inextricably intertwined. We will look at some of the fascinating gardens that he has created, both alone and in collaboration with James van Sweden. But it is impossible, when confronted with this tangled mass of garden and man, to show just the gardens. I must paint the portrait of a man, a strange, enigmatic man, and for many a mysterious and exotic personality. This perhaps explains the praise and fame that has come to a man who neither speaks nor writes much, doesn't move in influential circles, is neither particularly charming nor wordly, who doesn't even look brilliant or possess any of the other attributes usually needed to become a success.

He is driven on by an unquenchable passion for a vanished world, one that maybe never was. By the end of the book we will discover what might survive this man of the garden, what will continue to grow when he no longer pulls weeds by torchlight in his home town of Towson, when I no longer write books, and when you no longer read them.

But slowly, all in good time.

A happy child in the garden
The Chemnitz and Bitterfeld years

Left: Wolfgang Oehme comes from a middle class background. His mother was a housewife and worked in a factory as a young woman. His father worked for the Chemnitz Police Administration until he was transferred, against his will, to Bitterfeld.

Right: Most surviving photographs show the young Oehme in the Chemnitz allotment garden. His parents and relatives ensured an early affinity with the garden with a sandbox and small fish pond.

With over 700 goals to his name, Erwin Helmchen is one of the all time great German soccer players. His hat trick for Chemnitz Police FC in 1934 against Real Madrid is now legendary. Helmchen would occasionally visit Wissmannhof, an estate with a large central courtyard, to the great delight of the young boys who lived there. With their ball at his feet, it was every boy's dream to save one of his shots. All except one. Whenever a game started at Wissmannhof, he would pick up his tortoise and quietly take himself off to somewhere safer. This boy was Wolfgang Oehme. Born on the 18th of May 1930, he grew up at Wissmannhof. Even then he was an eccentric, playing in the sandpit alone or with his friend Dietmar

Kummer, or, aged just six, helping dig over the garden at the Knappteich allotments. Not for Wolfgang the soccer games, knock down ginger or other childish pranks. His father had sustained a stomach injury during the First World War and the family changed to a vegetarian diet, with fruit playing an important role. Once a week Wolfgang was dispatched to an aunt's large orchard, returning with 20 kilograms of cherries or whatever else was in season – a journey that entailed a two hour bike ride before catching the train back to Chemnitz. A considerable part of their fare came from their allotment and from the age of seven Wolfgang cultivated his own plot, with his Uncle Richard building a small pond for his fishes, frogs and tortoises. The allotment and the countryside round Knappteich were the preserve of this solitary boy. The voluntary separation from his peers, which would normally provide fun and security, is difficult to understand. These missed childhood experiences would later haunt Wolfgang, and even in old age leave him searching for fulfilment.

Wolfgang followed his instincts, and tried to make life as easy as possible for his parents. He saw the need to put enough food on the table as a sacred task rather than a burden, even at primary school age. He often headed to the allotment for produce as times became more difficult during the war. Here, at the same time, he experienced the wonders of nature. A savoy cabbage could grow from a tiny seed, and if he had dug in some of

Wolfgang Oehme grew up an only child in Chemnitz. Although this group of solemn relatives might indicate otherwise, his childhood memories are mostly happy ones.

This photo shows Wolfgang in his first job, as an apprentice in Bitterfeld in the nursery of Max Illge.

the horse manure that he collected from nearby streets, it could grow to be a large savoy cabbage. But it would only flourish with constant weeding. To weed was to protect your food. Soon Wolfgang was weeding his neighbours' allotments too, earning him praise and encouragement. If you take a stroll with Oehme through his parks and gardens today, you'll be amazed by his ever-vigilant gaze, still searching for weeds and plucking them out, giving us a glimpse into his childhood.

But it wasn't all work and even the eccentric Wolfgang found ways to escape his self-imposed duties and responsibilities. He enjoyed going to the cinema, and watching documentaries gave him dreams of living in Africa, trips to the circus a chance to laugh at his favourite animals, the playful chimps. Then it was back to feed worms to his tortoises, fishes and frogs, and to sing songs from operettas to the horses in the field nearby.

He had to say farewell to all this – the animals, the allotment and his sandpit friend Dietmar Kummer, when his father was transferred to Bitterfeld in 1943. There was no allotment, just a garden behind the rented house at number 11 Richard Wagner Street. After school, he would garden here, before losing himself in the exciting, exotic world of Karl May novels. The bleak war and post-war years brought hunger and loss, and destruction to houses and gardens. Wolfgang remembers Bitterfeld at the end of the war very well. 'The town was totally overgrown, weeds were everywhere. Weeding was essential for survival: the weeds were either edible or they deprived cultivated plants of space and nutrients.' Leaving school in 1947, he had only one plan – to become a gardener. His first training was at the Illge Nursery. First and foremost they grew food plants, ornamental plants came a distant second. Cabbages, beans and potatoes were all very familiar to the apprentice, and most of what he wanted to learn had to wait until after work. His first opportunity for designing gardens, independently creating living spaces for plants and animals, came when he joined the Bitterfeld Parks and Cemeteries Department. Here, the landscape architect Hans-Joachim Bauer became his boss and mentor, and Oehme owes him a debt of gratitude. Bauer shared his time and expertise with the young gardener, and drove him around visiting gardens and parks. You can well imagine that Bauer had never had someone so thirsty for knowledge, so committed to becoming a gardener in his care. And it was Bauer who introduced his protégé to an even more influential figure – Karl Foerster, the great gardener from Bornim near Potsdam. It was also Bauer who recommended that Oehme study garden design in Dahlem. The Bitterfeld Parks and Cemeteries Department could have become his home, but instead proved to be just a springboard to Berlin.

Out of East Germany
Study and experience

Crossing Maryland under a stormy sky, the flatlands east of Chesapeake Bay, green fades to grey, brown to black, and farm buildings blur behind the torrential rain. The wind would blow the car off course without a firm hand on the wheel. The other hand is conducting, while the choir sings 'Freude, schöner Götterfunken, Tochter aus Elysium, Wir betreten feuertrunken, Himmlische, dein Heiligtum.' (Joy, bright spark of divinity, Daughter of Elysium, fire inspired we tread Thy sanctuary.)

Beethoven – Wolfgang Oehme's constant companion for almost sixty years. Oehme's interest in poetry, drama and music began in Bitterfeld, with Goethe, Heine and Schiller offering him a glimpse of freedom from the boredom of provincial life in a small mining town. Beethoven provided a rousing score for these stirring lyrics, and perhaps encouraged Wolfgang to dream in larger dimensions. The first significant change to his vision came one spring day in 1952. His parents had long thought that their son's free spirit would be stifled by the narrow confines of the GDR, and Wolfgang had applied successfully for a place at the Advanced School of Garden Design in Dahlem, and for a grant from West Germany. So on that spring morning, he set off on his heavily-laden bike, with a few marks in his pocket and his parents waving him off. He was heading not yet for Dahlem, his course only started in the autumn, but for the Baumschulenweg in Berlin and the Späth nursery, rich in tradition but already at this time property of the citizens of the GDR. He cycled through the destroyed city, stunned and shocked, and soon found himself in the yard at Späth's. He wanted to work. And to learn. It didn't take him long to become the firm's fastest rose-grafter.

In the autumn he took up his place at the Advanced School of Garden Design. Here in Dahlem he saw ornamental grasses in 'lavish, almost wasteful plenty', as he put it. His favourite subjects were physics and outdoor plants, but he had little enthusiasm for chemistry or freehand drawing. Nothing much has changed in that regard. Wolfgang Oehme was and is a practical gardener; he wants to plant trees and perennials, not draw them; to dig the hole there and then, not enter it neatly on to the plans. As a break from their studies, he and his friend Inge Richter went to operas and concerts. 'Freude, schöner Götterfunken ... alle Menschen werden Brüder.' (Joy, bright spark of divinity ... all men become brothers.)

As a student Oehme still had not become one of the crowd. He avoided loud parties and preferred events with just a few people to whom he could relate. When not in lectures, he spent most of his time with a spade and secateurs. With the help of another friend, Adolf Singelmann, he got a job digging ditches at the 1953 International Garden Design Show in Hamburg. Helping to create new green spaces in bombed cities gave his career a great new significance. Much has changed

since then but he still feels a close connection with the Planten un Blomen gardens. He lists them among his five favourite places on earth, and the then head of planning, Karl Plomin, among his five most admired people. Plomin made widespread use of *Calamagrostis* x *acutiflora* 'Karl Foerster' (feather reed grass), and Oehme's experience here was to have a profound effect on his future. He then went to work in Sweden with his fellow student Rolf Schmidt, and only returned well after the beginning of the new term. The staff at the School of Garden Design were used to this, as many students took time out to do paid work for their former employers. Oehme had been living in the Soviet Zone, but in 1953 he moved to the western part of the city, accompanied

by the noise of thunderous tanks. To return to East Germany was unthinkable. He now settled in the land that had supported him through his lean student years: a programme of similar grants contributed considerably to the brain drain from East Germany, thus undermining the government there. In 1954 Oehme graduated as a garden design technician, with the option of completing his Masters degree at a later stage.

Having graduated, he headed for the home of the horticulture, and spent a year at Waterer Sons & Crisp, a nursery in Bagshot, just south of London. Here he learned English, quite unaware of the role it would play in his life. His first job as a planner in Germany was in the Gardens Department in Frankfurt am Main, before moving in spring 1956 to the landscape architects Delius in Nürnberg. He didn't stay long. Later that summer at an international conference he met American University Professor Hubert Owens, and from that moment could hardly wait to start a new life in the New World. He lived in Nürnberg until the 19th of January 1957 when he moved to Baltimore. He took the *Ode to Joy* with him. 'Alle Menschen werden Brüder, ... Freude trinken alle Wesen, An den Brüsten der Natur, Alle Guten, alle Bösen, Folgen ihrer Rosenspur.' (All men become brothers, ... All creatures drink of joy, at nature's breast. Just and unjust alike taste of her gift.)

Left: Oehme acquired the theoretical foundations of landscape architecture and garden design at the Advanced School of Garden Design in Berlin. This picture shows him (right) in 1953 with fellow students Ekkehart Schmidt and Eva Schlothauer.

Below: After graduating, Wolfgang was on the move, first to Waterer Sons & Crisp in Surrey. Here we see him celebrating Christmas 1954 in grand style with three German exchange students.

To be a Foersteranian
The message of the great gardener from Bornim

Still behind the Iron Curtain, Eva Foerster wrote to Wolfgang Oehme in 1987: 'Grasses! Grasses! I'm sure you know the wonderful new *Miscanthus sinensis* varieties 'Malepartus', 'Rotsilber', 'Silberfeder' – you can get them all from Countess Zeppelin's nursery in West Germany.' The widow of the renowned perennial grower and author, Karl Foerster, who had died seventeen years before, had become a passionate gardener, and was very keen to pass on sources for her favourite plants. Even to America. Wolfgang gilded their correspondence with seeds and other gifts from the plant life of the New World, always eager to keep in contact with the gardening family from Bornim. One parcel arrived from America, large but very light, filled with seeds from *Pennisetum orientale*, 'enough for several nurseries', Karl's daughter, Marianne, noted at the time.

For Wolfgang Oehme, Karl Foerster is more than just a plantsman – he is a force of nature, and an enormous influence on his life and work. Oehme still turns the pages of a yellowed 1939 nursery catalogue as eagerly as if it were filled with maps for buried treasure. 'The Foerster catalogue – that was our bible,' he tells a friend who discovers the Advanced School of Garden Design's sacred plant book on his shelves.

The old Foerster catalogues give us just a hint of why a new breed of gardener emerged in the first half of the twentieth century; Foersteranians. In his books as well as his catalogues Foerster formulated his very own

philosophy of gardening and nature. A like-minded tribe gathered in Bornim to work for a better world, within the framework of this new outlook. Amongst those in this group were Gottfried Kühn, Richard Hansen and Alfred Reich, and also Heinz Hagemann and Ernst Pagels, who had been taught propagation and garden design by Foerster. What captivated Wolfgang Oehme as a young man were Foerster's thoughts, that you are deeply rooted in the earth, intimately connected to the plant as your material, but at the same time woven into the fabric of the commonplace, adaptable to all attitudes, sometimes humorous, sometimes reflective, usually full of optimism. Oehme felt in tune with Foerster from the first day he heard and read about him, but circumstances after the war made it difficult to get to know this great man better. Had he been born at the right time, he would have given everything to become a Foerster disciple. For Oehme there is no better model.

Foerster's hasty jottings were taken as his maxims. 'Blooming during all seasons' became his manifesto, and he created the idea of a season for America's gardens in which grasses bloom, or together with herbaceous perennials carry their thousands of seeds into winter. It is this 'seventh season' that best differentiates Oehme from most other gardeners. He has given Foerster's book *Einzug der Farne und Gräser in die Gärten* (Grasses and ferns in the garden) to literally hundreds of his clients, regardless of whether or not they can read it. His own

Above: Wolfgang Oehme corresponded for many years with Eva, Karl Foerster's wife.

Top Right: Wolfgang and Marianne Foerster in Bornim, on his visit to Germany in 1991.

Opposite: Karl Foerster, without doubt the biggest influence on Oehme, and without whom he might never have found his vocation. Oehme has the greatest respect for his achievements, and also for his attitude of mind.

copy, published in 1957, is now falling apart.

Foerster's view of humanity struck deep chord with Oehme and he rapidly found himself taken in by Foerster's outlook on life. 'Even the smallest effort to make a good impression can spoil everything. Only if the personality is truly and fully behind an idea can other effects come into play.' This spoke just as much to the socially awkward Oehme as to the gardener within him who wrestled with the tension between nature and artifice, foliage and weed, and for whom this idea became a lasting experience. 'The free-spirited gardener of today is entering into a new, adventurous marriage with nature.' Every day, at home or in the gardens of his clients, Wolfgang Oehme experiences these words by Foerster: 'the flower in the garden has shown itself to be a great pioneer of the new relationship between soul and world, more than we can know. Gardens and flowers have an unimaginable effect on us.'

Volkmar Wentzel, the famous *National Geographic* photographer, wrote in the journal *Museum and Arts Washington*, 'Like friendship, the development of a garden needs patience and understanding. At the beginning of this century, Karl Foerster sowed the seeds of a concept which Wolfgang Oehme has transplanted to America. And this concept has been brought to full bloom thanks to his partnership with James van Sweden.' Foerster was indeed the first to make tall grasses and perennials the centerpiece of the garden, and so must be described as the father of modern planting, imitative of and inspired by nature. In Foerster's *Grässlich ein Garten ohne Gräser* (Ghastly a garden without grasses) Wolfgang Oehme discovered a mission, and in America he found the dimensions to fulfill this mission.

The sunken garden at Bornim was already a Mecca
for garden designers when Oehme was at college.
Lovingly preserved and developed by Marianne Foerster,
the entire garden is part of the Potsdam Sanssouci World
Heritage Site.

Take off and landing
A new start in America

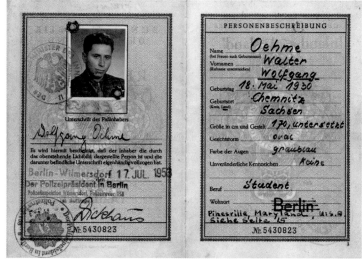

In his years of travelling, Wolfgang Oehme proved to himself that he could adapt to foreign ground. From that point of view he was emotionally well prepared for his departure from Germany. In 1957 the turboprop airliner had to refuel three times – in Ireland, Iceland and Newfoundland – before arrival in New York. From Idlewild, now the John F. Kennedy International Airport, Wolfgang made his way to Manhattan, then by train to Baltimore. A year later, Wolfgang visited Germany after a bout of homesickness, and then returned to Baltimore, having first bought a Volkswagen, which he had shipped to America. This was the year that saw the leading travel writer Wolfgang Koeppen visit the United States, following Oehme's route. His memories of that train journey can be read in his *American Journey*. He was impressed by the thunderstorms, compared to which the German variety seemed tame, and by nature at the roadside, never mastered and often threatening to engulf the domesticated and motorized Americans. Leaving the train in Washington Koeppen had arrived in the south; the air hit him like 'a slap with a heavy, steaming towel'. Wolfgang Oehme left his train in the neighbouring city of Baltimore, without concern for the weather or vegetation. He would just have to get on with this new climate, this was home now, even if it was never entirely meant to be.

Opposite left: Initially Wolfgang Oehme landed in New York. After the construction of the TWA Terminal in 1962, designed by Eero Saarinen, he left Idlewild Airport through the doors of one of the most impressive airport buildings in the world.

Opposite right: A dream becomes reality for the young man who grew up in provincial Germany. Berlin has been replaced by Pikesville, Maryland as his place of residence; Oehme is now a US citizen.

Right: As a child Wolfgang devoured books by Karl May. But he soon realised that the domestic arrangements of Native Americans had changed, and that tepees were a thing of the past.

Oehme had come to Baltimore on the recommendation of the renowned college professor Hubert Owens. They had got to know each other in Zürich at a conference in August 1956, after which Owens secured a job for the twenty-six year old with the landscape designer Bruce Baetjer in Baltimore. He spent Christmas with his family in East Germany, before flying to New York in January 1957. He had achieved his dream of leaving the provincial, often small-minded Germany behind and set out to conquer the world. Some dreams contain surprises: one lunchtime he was disappointed to learn from his colleague William Dreyer, still a good friend, that Red Indians in full traditional dress were not to be found. Not a minute later a colourfully painted Native American appeared, part of a government delegation. An avid fan of Karl May, the famous German writer of Wild West stories, Oehme was somewhat surprised at the sight of red and white getting on so well. America was not all as he had anticipated, which left the young German, so keen to develop his ideas, with more of a challenge; just as remote as tepees and pueblos, bows and arrows, were the plants, found in Germany and assumed to be here. The towering perennials and grasses of the prairies were nowhere to be seen on the East Coast. Instead the New World greeted him with trees, scattered on endless carpets of grass, and with this spreading evergreen, manicured block of vegetation alongside windowsill or veranda, came the so-called 'foundation planting'. Nearly all buildings had this green pedestal, all the front gardens in the suburbs blurring together in a green monotone, they looked like public parks, with no individuality and required a huge amount of care; cutting, aerating, weeding, watering, feeding – too much effort for lifeless green boredom. Oehme the pacifist had an enemy – lawn!

In the eighteen months he spent with Bruce Baetjer, Wolfgang was already trying to find alternatives to all this lawn. When Baetjer closed his business, Oehme moved to the safer environs of a planning authority, to Baltimore County, having already started to create his own gardens. He worked there until 1966, and had the opportunity to teach at the University of Pennsylvania and then the University of Georgia.

In 1966 he went freelance, so at last he could work as he wished, as his own master. His commissions ranged from extensive park complexes to small private gardens. Even at this early stage, there was not a speck of lawn to be seen in the domestic gardens he created. Stone, gravel, pool, with familiar and alien plants in between – this was Oehme's signature. All this aroused general interest in the neighbourhoods, and he had plenty of recommendations, but he was still regarded suspiciously by his professional peers. In a letter of thanks after a lecture at a garden society in the mid-60s, he read 'some of the audience seemed to be rather skeptical about your enthusiasm for ornamental grasses.' Far from disillusioned, this served merely to inspire him further. In a contemporary pamphlet of rules and regulations

The proud owner of a Morris Minor, his first car.
Acquired in just his first year as a garden designer, it was
soon replaced with a VW Squareback, imported
from Germany.

Oehme was already designing gardens in the early 1960s,
alongside his job in the local planning department.
His ideas were unheard of in America, but word soon
spread through his neighbourhood in Pikesville.

Wolfgang lectured on the use of plants at the
University of Georgia in the 60s. This picture shows
his Volkswagen outside the house of a professor who
commissioned him to design the University garden.

Initially, Wolfgang Oehme replaced lawns with
exposed concrete slabs dotted with the few perennials
and grasses available at the time. Even in 1959, a pool
was very much part of the American dream house.

he noted one passage in particular, about 'domestic improvements', and the very clear advice that the drive, veranda, fence, pool and landscaping were all part of these improvements. For Oehme the improvements lay primarily in herbaceous perennials and grasses.

The 60s were above all a time to learn. Here in the humid south, the landscape could be compared with central Europe, but the climate was very different. Many familiar plants struggled to survive or were unobtainable and he had to add many alien ones to his repertoire. Just about every Sunday was spent studying or out in the country, where he would dig up wild plants for his gardens. Well stocked nurseries, a basic requirement for his professional survival, were still to be built and

fed with seeds. In front of him lay a wide, empty field that needed to be attacked from all sides and with all manner of tools. He was certain that ignorance was to blame for the wastelands that Americans dared to call their gardens. Miserable lawns, kept short by amateurs with lawnmowers, had to give way to gardens, tended by gardeners. Something had to done.

The first masterpiece
The Vollmer Garden, Baltimore, Maryland

Above: Now over ninety, Pauline Vollmer was amongst the first to sacrifice her lawn in favour of perennials and trees, and was very much responsible, with her husband, for spreading Oehme's gardening philosophy.

Opposite: Knotweed, hostas and *Miscanthus* were almost unknown in the US forty years ago. Wolfgang attracted attention with his use of robust shrubs like *Photinia villosa*, and extravagant trees.

Pioneers, for Americans the first families that set out with their covered wagons across the prairies, conquered the Rocky Mountains and found space to live in the land beyond. Wolfgang Oehme was also searching for space to live. But for him it was less about his own piece of land and a place to settle, and more about self-realisation, whether on his own land or someone else's was not important. For this he needed souls who were unsatisfied with their own patch of lawn, entrusting it to him and hoping for the best. It wasn't just Oehme who was a pioneer; his clients had to be daring in giving him their land. They had little idea how their gardens would look once Oehme had them in his hands. Without computer-generated images, or even the skills of an artist or gifted speaker, Oehme could only give the faintest idea of his vision. And even if his descriptive powers were good enough – what would the neighbours say?

At this point, we must mention two names: Pauline and Leo Vollmer. Both have played a significant part in Wolfgang's life. Pauline, now over ninety, continued in this role after Leo's death in 1987. The Vollmers were typical Americans, inasmuch as they had a substantial amount of money to spend on charitable projects. And on gardening. Their enthusiasm and involvement started with their own garden in Maryland, which as usual comprised trees, bushes and lawn. Wolfgang Oehme and his friend Kurt Bluemel were recommended to them, and a meeting was arranged. Bluemel had been in the

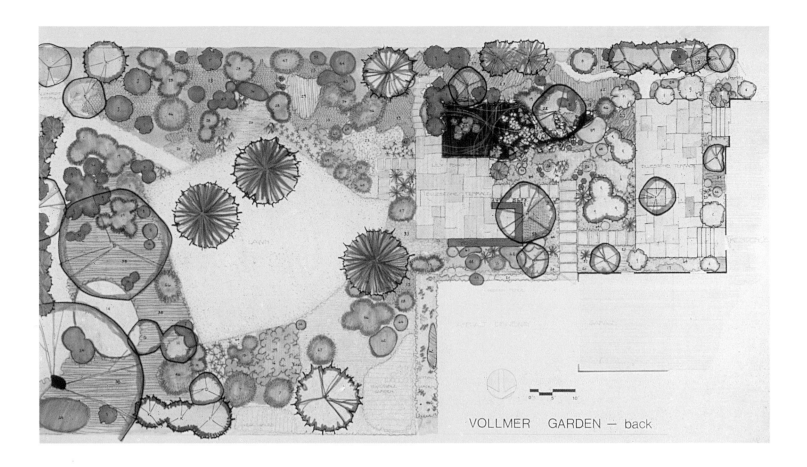

VOLLMER   GARDEN — back

USA since 1960, and by the mid-60s was working with Oehme. Wolfgang's success can really be dated from the time the remodelling of the Vollmer's garden began.

Journals and newspapers started to take notice of this garden, his first masterpiece. Leo Vollmer became a central figure in the project, hitching himself to the partnership by buying some land for Kurt Bluemel to establish a nursery. In turn, Bluemel was to become Oehme's plant supplier in the years and decades to come. Pauline Vollmer was also a driving force, constantly active on Wolfgang's behalf in gardening societies and clubs, and responsible for creating a network of potential clients. She doted on the curious German, and for many years organised birthday parties for her 'Wülfgang' in her garden. Without the Vollmers everything would probably have been very different, and success would have been much harder to achieve.

'It's taken a while to get used to the new garden. My husband wanted a fishpond, which he got. I wanted roses, which I got but had to get rid of again, as pesticides and fish don't go well together. It has turned out so well, I wouldn't swap it for any other,' Pauline Vollmer explains. Bit by bit, over many years, Oehme replaced the lawn with herbaceous perennials, initially in the front garden, then the back garden. It has now all matured wonderfully. The upper terrace by the house and the lower one around the small fishpond have been harmoniously united by small trees, shrubs, herbaceous perennials and grasses. The mastery of the slope, the correct proportions of solid ground and vegetation, and the relatively muted use of plants (in comparison to later projects) all explain why visitors are still entranced, even forty years after its

creation. All 2,000 square metres can never been seen in their entirety – something is always blocking the view. But the rear, or lower, garden does not give the impression of a gloomy, dark thicket, but is more of an invitation to plunge along the narrow path for some botanical surprises. Pauline Vollmer still finds something new to delight her on her daily walk along this path. 'We don't like to go on vacation quite so much since we've had this garden,' she comments. 'We just couldn't go away in spring when the dogwood is in blossom, in summer and autumn when the ornamental grasses shimmer so beautifully, and in the winter when all the seedpods are covered in frost. This garden has really changed my life.' And not just her life.

Above: The view drops away from the ground floor, over the long upper terrace down to the lower, square seating area. A redwood wall clad with slats separates the upper areas, and encloses the L-shaped terrace on two sides.

Opposite: The plans for the Vollmer's back garden. The lawn between terrace and thicket at the bottom of the garden is still shown, but even this has given way over the years to grasses and perennials.

Above and right: Pauline Vollmer's garden captivates us with, on the one hand a convincingly formal basic structure, and on the other with its thrilling confusion that never quite descends into chaos. The huge variety of plants ensures a constantly changing picture. Trees and perennials selected for their longevity only grow to medium height, ensuring that even after forty years the proportions are still perfectly balanced.

Perennials for America
The creation of a plant collection for Wolfgang Oehme

Above: This book with its hidden compartment travelled with Oehme for years, but is now a happy memory of the time in which thousands of seeds made their well-camouflaged way across the Atlantic to satisfy the thirst for perennials in the USA.

Opposite: Two men, past retirement age, who just can't let go. Wolfgang with the celebrated gardener and plantsman Kurt Bluemel, whose life's work is also bringing grasses and perennials to America.

Success has many fathers. When Wolfgang Oehme arrived in the USA he could count on two hands the number of herbaceous perennials available for him to use in his gardens. Uncut grasses were only to be found by the roadside, on the prairies and in just a few old gardens, but were nowhere to be seen in newly designed ones. That hundreds of varieties of ornamental grass are now available is thanks to just a few individuals, Oehme amongst them. No botanic garden or nursery in Germany was safe in the 50s, 60s and 70s from his eager eyes, forever on the lookout for new seeds. His relatives were roped in too, like his cousin Frank, who in 1963 sent him the reed grass *Calamagrostis* x *acutiflora* 'Stricta' from Denmark, which was to become one of the favourite ornamental grasses in America. But Oehme needed plants in vast quantities, he needed allies. Amongst these, one name stand out – Kurt Bluemel.

Born in 1933 in Bohemia, Kurt emigrated to the USA from Switzerland in 1960. 'My love for ornamental grasses started at Vogt's perennial nursery by the Zürichsee. It was a real shock to discover that here in the USA they were regarded as wilderness plants. As Vogt was allowed to export to the US, I could slowly start to build up my range. But back then we were producing plants in the dark – there was no demand for them. I first met Wolfgang Oehme in the early 1960s at Richard Simon's Bluemount Nursery, where he bought

his plants. He was constantly encouraging me to import and propagate grasses. Importing plants to the USA was always complicated and strictly controlled, but over the years I managed to build up an impressive collection, mainly thanks to Vogt. I got *Calamagrostis* x *acutiflora* 'Karl Foerster' from there, without which garden design as nature intended would be unthinkable. Wolfgang and I became friends, and until we started our own businesses worked together to create herbaceous perennial and grass gardens. For years my company was the sole source of grasses, perennials and specialist trees for Wolfgang, and later Wolfgang and his partner James van Sweden. Alex and Carole Rosenberg's garden on Long Island gave me a big helping hand, as it needed great quantities of perennials and grasses. The widespread publicity it

received turned it into a kind of model garden for me. And now Wolfgang and I are pensioners, but we just can't stop gardening, and he is still using my plants in his gardens.'

But you would be doing Kurt Bluemel an injustice by saying he is just the owner of a firm that grows plants for garden designers. He creates gardens himself, testing and showing the possibilities of the plants in situ. Above all, he has the necessary enthusiasm and pioneering spirit to bring unknown and sometimes surprising plants into the mainstream. His enthusiasm is apparent in his lectures, in his contributions to many books, and in his work as president of a wide variety of associations. For many years his nursery has been an inspirational if temporary employer for German gardeners and students.

His enquiring mind has led to the introduction of many grasses, some of which have also found their way over to Europe. 'Adagio', 'Allegro' and 'Rigoletto' are some of his varieties of *Miscanthus sinensis*. *Panicum virgatum* 'Heavy Metal', 'Warrior' and 'Squaw' come from his nursery, as well as *Pennisetum* varieties 'Foxtrot', 'Moudry' and 'Cassian' and *Molinia caerulea* subsp. *arundinacea* 'Skyracer' and 'Jazz'. Legend has it that many of these plants are dedicated to his wife Hannah. She is, of course, a musician.

Above: Bluemel developed a particular love for ornamental grasses. As well as multiplying already available varieties, over the years he began propagating his own varieties, including *Pennisetum* 'Moudry'.

Opposite: Kurt Bluemel founded his nursery in 1964. Oehme has his commitment and daring to thank for being able to realise his vision for garden design so rapidly.

Solo no more
Collaboration with James van Sweden

What is happiness? When, in the same moment, the will and the deed merge? At least, as Herman Melville wrote, one is able to avoid a terrible fate. Rarely do we meet someone for whom the will and the deed do merge, for whom an imbalance would lead to disaster. Wolfgang Oehme is one such person. While he was pondering all this, and how his days were unavoidably filled with the spirit of Karl Foerster, another man was suffering the consequences of this imbalance, stuck in a town planner's office. He was James van Sweden.

He met Oehme in the early 60s and saw how he could turn a rapidly sketched design into a finished garden, how his hands transformed the environment and how that piece of land could bring both little joys and great happiness. It was different for him – plans could take years to complete, and then disappear back into the drawers from which they had come. Over the years Jim helped his friend now and then with his gardens, but not until 1975 did they open an office together in Washington DC, about 50 kilometres south of Baltimore. The attraction of this partnership was not obvious to everyone: Oehme, the taciturn, shy loner, and van Sweden, the genial socialiser – it wouldn't last long. But it has, and is still going strong. It is precisely this contrasting work approach that has given them freedom without any boundaries. Van Sweden commented, 'I can learn a lot from Wolfgang.' Oehme said, 'with Jim we can make a real success of this business.' These

Opposite: James van Sweden's garden in Washington was their first joint project, which became a living brochure for the company they founded there.

Below: Their rapid success led them to move their offices from Georgetown to Capitol Hill. Years later and again short of space, they added the white house next door. OvS currently employs a staff of thirty.

convictions were strengthened by the gardens that Oehme, and sometimes the two of them, created, which drew considerable attention. They were already using van Sweden's own small garden in Georgetown as a three-dimensional portfolio.

The breakthrough did not, however, come with a private garden. In 1976 a senior figure at the Federal Reserve Bank on Pennsylvania Avenue in Washington read a newspaper article about Oehme and his gardens. A cold winter had destroyed almost all their plants, and a new layout was needed. They wanted an area of more human dimensions to surround this massive stronghold of American finance, to inspire private thoughts, for leisure time and play. The article about Oehme

brought the promise of a completely new perspective. Private gardens, as long as the planting was large-scale and generous, could also serve as a model for public parks. And so the first really ambitious work by Oehme and van Sweden (known in the trade as OvS) came into being. *Rudbeckia fulgida* 'Goldsturm' stormed between *Miscanthus sedum telephium* 'Herbstfreude' or 'Autumn Joy' and *Pennisetum* formed great fields of colour and wound between the trunks of cherry trees, whilst the background was illuminated by groupings of the reed grass *Calamagrostis*. This was all totally new. It hadn't been seen before, even in Germany. From Potsdam Eva Foerster wrote enthusiastically, 'well, you two are really excited about your grasses. This garden is so lovely, so

impressive – and now the cat-woman's creation too, startlingly beautiful.' The cat-woman was the artist Lila Katzen, who had erected an abstract steel sculpture in the garden. The contrast was sensational. Lila Katzen was soon to play a quite unintentional role in the meteoric rise of the design duo.

The new garden at the Bank fitted perfectly into the plans for upgrading Pennsylvania Avenue between the Federal Reserve building and the National Gallery. The new look was to be continued. OvS was in business. This was a dream come true for Wolfgang Oehme – contrary to popular belief, public parks are very close to his heart. They provide recreation for many, and also inspiration for their own gardens, at least in Oehme's

opinion. 'Instead of just a boring park, we have created a botanical garden for the masses,' he commented for the record in his reserved mumble. Lavish plantings transformed the wide variety of open spaces along this great avenue, and also in Pershing Park, created in 1976 by landscape designer Paul Friedberg right in front of the luxurious Willard Intercontinental Hotel. Banks and stepped terraces ingeniously protect this oasis from the traffic, but the dominant juniper and ivy gave it a rather melancholy atmosphere. Friedberg was only mildly impressed when his cemetery plants were replaced by grasses, perennials and deciduous trees, bringing colour and seasonal variation to the park. As the new planting developed, Friedberg changed his mind: 'we made a vase,

and OvS has filled it with flowers.'

Around this time, Oehme and van Sweden caused a buzz elsewhere in the capital too. On a great slope, between embassies and other office buildings, the team created a garden landscape which drew people from far and wide, as a great place to relax. It was here that extensive groupings of *Rudbeckia fulgida* 'Goldsturm', *Panicum virgatum* 'Haense Herms' and *Sedum telephium* 'Autumn Joy' became their trademark. Henry Mitchell, in his well known *Washington Post* gardening column, hit the nail on the head: 'I wouldn't be at all surprised to see a lion peering out of Oehme van Sweden's grasslands. The gardens of OvS are quite magical (without the

lions), and here the foolishness of the accepted rules becomes apparent. The trick is an almost total absence of the usual flowers – peonies, iris, lilies etc, and instead far more trouble-free plants that hardly need any care.' Until then nature, or even worse wilderness, and the American garden just did not go together. But now, with the idea of a distinct, danger-free wilderness, a door was opened for all those who yearned for a wild, or at least wide open America, the land of their forefathers. Many thousands of *Rudbeckia* plants, mixed with prairie grasses, painted an impressive picture of the North American landscape, not wild but looking like it, natural but under control.

The commission to design the German-American Friendship Garden in a prominent location between the White House and the Washington Monument was made to measure for Oehme. Created in memory of the first German immigrants who arrived 300 years previously, many fleeing religious persecution to begin a new life, it was an honour for the free-thinking Oehme to design this garden around an oak tree planted by the President of West Germany Karl Carstens in 1983. Officially dedicated by Heads of State Kohl and Reagan in 1988, the design, the site supervision and the plants were all donated by OvS. Every year some seven million people relax in this tranquil spot, cooling their foreheads and feet

Above: The open spaces in the consular quarter of Washington bear the unmistakeable stamp of Oehme and van Sweden. The reproduction of a natural landscape in an urban setting was a sensation.

Opposite: Pershing Park was originally planted with mostly dark evergreens. OvS changed the mood completely with grasses, perennials and deciduous trees.

Left: Oehme and van Sweden designed the German-American Friendship Garden between the Washington Monument and the White House. Although right next to the expansive Mall, it has an intimate feel that is all its own.

Opposite: Commissions for public parks came from outside Washington too. The civilised wilderness at Battery Park City has enhanced the backdrop of skyscrapers along the Hudson for the last fifteen years.

in the simple fountains.

For many years thousands of *Miscanthus* stems have also been rustling in the breeze in America's unofficial capital. In 1992 OvS brought to fruition the biggest public park in Battery Park City in Manhattan, the Nelson A. Rockefeller Park. Mostly undamaged by the dreadful events of September 11th 2001 which so dramatically changed the backdrop, the land reclaimed from the Hudson River now provides space for ball parks, playgrounds, ornamental plants and a water lily pond on the upper level, whilst below are open spaces for playing and a more relaxed, meadow-like planting scheme. Because of the very heavy recreational use, Oehme has had to give way to the lawn. However, with their use of herbaceous perennials and grasses the designers have nonetheless managed to convey a hint of nature, matching the mood of the river on the edge of the overcrowded, unceasing activity of the financial district, and not least creating a charm that lasts all year. But this is not their only achievement in and around New York.

Made in Heaven
The Rosenberg Garden, Long Island, New York

Still in New York, we return to the cat-woman, Lila Katzen. Not long before she added her sculpture to the Federal Reserve Bank garden, art dealers Carole and Alex Rosenberg bought a weekend house on Long Island, the once modest spit of land just off Manhattan. Salvador Dalí, Henry Moore, Andy Warhol... the Rosenbergs had a lot of illustrious people in their address book. And under the letter K was Katzen.

The house on Long Island was lovely, but the garden unrecognisable as such, a tangled wilderness which ran from the house down to the waterline of Mecox Bay, and which soon fell victim to the Rosenberg's spades. But what then? Carole Rosenberg didn't want the typical American garden, she wanted something special, although she had no idea what. Just like the art she bought and sold, she had to like it, but it was up to someone else to make it. The Rosenbergs commissioned a local garden designer, who was so uninspired as to 'borrow' an artist's sketch for a pool, placing it right on the shore as part of his own plans. He departed soon thereafter. They were at a loss as to what to do next, and it came up at one of the many meetings art dealers have with artists. On this particular evening, Lila Katzen gave them a solution in just three letters – OvS. Carole Rosenberg was hesitant because of the 250 miles between Oehme van Sweden in Washington and Long Island, but James van Sweden wouldn't be put off, and came to see her with a beautiful design. It worked, and Carole reached for a pen. 'Where do I sign?' was her only question. The gardeners and Kurt Bluemel's plants arrived soon after. Oehme and van Sweden used familiar material and manpower, and the job was done in just a day and a half.

The garden initially looked like it had chicken pox, grins Alex Rosenberg today, but after just three years the individual strands of herbaceous perennials and grasses had grown together. For an American like Carole Rosenberg, who had only known the rigidity of lawn and tree, this was a miracle. 'I stood on the terrace,

Opposite: New York art dealers Carole and Alex Rosenberg commissioned the garden at their country house on Long Island twenty years ago. It has become a great piece of advertising for Oehme's art.

Below: The plans for the Rosenberg's garden are no longer quite accurate but show the rigid basic structure. Terraces, pool, perennials and grasses encircle the house, the carefully proportioned lawn ensures a clear view over Mecox Bay.

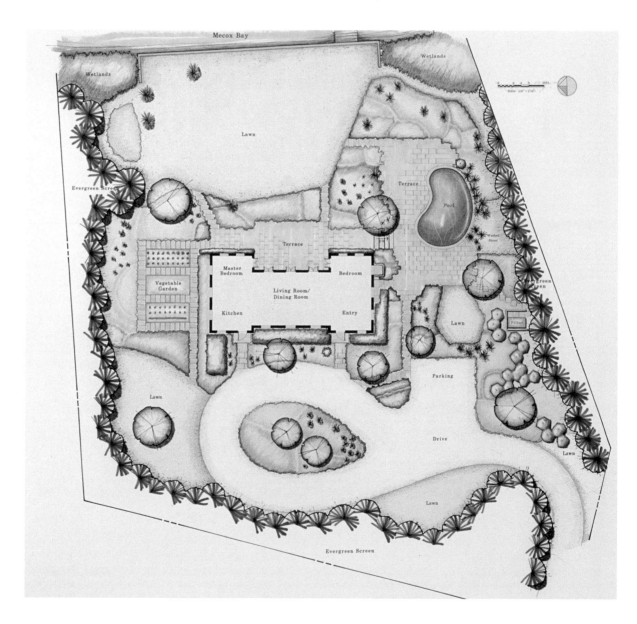

looked out at the bay over the grasses waving in the wind, and thought, yes, this garden looks like it was made in heaven.' One of the many visitors to the garden, thanking the Rosenbergs for their hospitality, wrote, 'I have never seen a garden in which nature and art have been brought together with so much love and respect.' A letter from the Pennsylvania Horticultural Society carried this to extremes: 'You have the perfect design and the perfect plants for the perfect place.' The fusion of garden and landscape has indeed worked brilliantly. A solid barrier of *Pennisetum alopecuroides* separates the terrace from the lawn running down to the bay, where two sculpture-like *Miscanthus* x *giganteus*, giant Chinese silver grass, stand. They never seem to intrude on the view over the water because they naturally form part of the overall picture. Behind the pool your eye is caught by a Henry Moore sculpture, and the terrace lifted by *Molinia caerulea* subsp. *arundinacea* 'Windspiel', elegant, spacious, playfully off-setting wind and weather. Long Island provides a relatively short growing season, as the ocean keeps the ground cool for a long period. This does not bother the summer-flowering grasses such as *Pennisetum*, *Miscanthus* and *Molinia*, as they do not start growing until April anyway. Between cutting back and sprouting, spring bulbs bring their own life and colour to the garden.

There have been plenty of visitors to the garden in its twenty-five years, including some of the gardening world's most important figures: Christopher Lloyd, Rosemary Verey and Penelope Hobhouse have all visited, along with countless journalists, making this one of the

Thanks to the cooling Atlantic, spring comes late to Long Island, but warmer seas ensure a long autumn. The reedgrass *Molinia caerulea* subsp. *arundinacea* 'Windspiel' is ideal for coastal gardens, with its tall stems constantly swaying in the breeze.

most popular private gardens open to the public in the US today. In the years up to 2000, at least fourteen books and twenty-three different magazines featured the garden. It has given impetus and roots to Oehme's work, difficult to separate from his personal life. Alex and Carole Rosenberg have become friends, whose lives could hardly be more different to Wolfgang's, but whose views on gardening are very much the same. Unlike Carole, the vegetation sometimes comes too close to the house for Alex's tastes. He once asked Wolfgang for his advice about moving some of the plants further away, only to receive the reply, with a curt gesture and mischievous grin, 'move the house!' Put it on stilts in the water for

all I care, he is alleged to have offered as a solution. At any rate the plants would stay where he had put them. Carole then got involved in the discussion, and no more was heard about it.

Above all, the garden became an open-air showroom. The Rosenbergs, already gallery owners, presented a botanical work of art, thereby helping to promote Oehme van Sweden. They could never have afforded better publicity than that provided by the journalists of the *New York Times* or *Time Magazine* and the exceptionally hospitable and media-friendly owners. The Rosenbergs also became firm friends with James van Sweden, hosting a cocktail party on the OvS designed roof terrace of their

Above: In spring the few sculptures in the garden are visible, disappearing in summer behind the towering grasses and perennials; art and nature in harmony.

Opposite: A barrier of *Miscanthus* separates the pool on the terrace from the bay. The wind is barely noticed, catching only the tops of the grasses, completing the perfect visual and acoustic scene.

Manhattan apartment to celebrate the publication of a new book. Events like this, whether in town or on Long Island, made waves. A longing for these heaven-sent landscapes in your own backyard spread through certain circles, and the work started to come to OvS, not vice versa. Like news of a miracle cure, the wealthy citizens of Long Island, and other areas, started to take notice of the newspaper reports of gardens à la Rosenberg. Members of prominent society wanted a 'New American Garden.' A brand was born. Thousands, even hundreds of thousands of herbaceous perennials and grasses found their way into the gardens of Oehme and van Sweden.

Above: The entrance offers a particular attraction from late summer to early winter: the over-hanging shoots of the false hemp *Datisca cannabina* both greet and say farewell to the visitor.

Left: On the lawn by the bay are two thick clumps of switch which grow into imposing plant sculptures every year. Originally there were three of these clumps, but two proved to have an even stronger effect.

Garden of Mrs S.

In great swathes, the false hemp *Datisca cannabina* has put out its 3 metre long shoots. On their ends the seedpods, hanging by long threads, resemble small curtains or flags waving in the sea breeze. *Datisca cannabina* is a wonderful plant for welcoming and bidding farewell, at its best in large front gardens. Leaving the Rosenberg's house on Long Island, we are to visit a handful of gardens created by OvS since the 1980s. Even covering a small part of America means driving hundreds of miles. But the next garden isn't all that far away. Mrs S. lives quite close to the Rosenbergs, and we can spot her garden from the street. Beginning at the drive, towering grasses greet the visitor and accompany them up to the house. Oehme and van Sweden like to make their mark right at the gate. If at all possible front and back gardens should merge to create a sense of spaciousness. Most front gardens in this country need a sign saying 'garden'. They look like cemeteries, growls Oehme to himself. He then turns to his grasses, *Miscanthus*, *Pennisetum* and *Calamagrostis*, with their beige and silver seed pods, strides along a narrow path through a lake of *Amsonia hubrichtii*, arrives at the back of the house and finds himself in a sea of *Lysimachia clethroides*. All these plants are swept back and forth by the constant sea breeze, with thousands of rust-red stonecrop flowers remaining upright in between. Both the leaf texture and its rigidity make *Sedum telephium* 'Autumn Joy' so valuable as a contrast to its neighbours blowing in the

Garden of Mrs S.

Opposite: Even without a view of the nearby Atlantic, Oehme and van Sweden have created a wonderfully maritime mood. In the back garden (left) thousands of gooseneck loosestrife *Lysimachia clethroides* billow elegantly in the wind. Diving into the pool here, you feel as if in another world. Just a narrow path leads from the driveway and front garden to the rear of the house, through lavish spreads of stonecrop *Sedum telephium* 'Autumn Joy' and *Amsonia hubrichtii* (right), with robust *Miscanthus* and mid-height shrubs and trees growing through them. This intertwining of plants may look natural, but takes real skill to achieve.

wind. We take the same path back, only visible when one is right on top of it, otherwise lost in the sea of grass.

Garden of Mr and Mrs H.

Staying on Long Island before heading for distant Pennsylvania, a light lunch is suggested ahead of our visit to Mr and Mrs H's garden. But Wolfgang won't hear of it. He has trained himself to go without food for hours without getting hungry. The hunger for his gardens must always be satisfied first – after that, what will be will be. But today he gives in easily, and generously passes round a jute bag. Wolfgang the bear, as he calls himself, grabs an apple in his solid paw, Wolfgang the lion bites straight into the top of the apple, not the side like

Garden of Mr and Mrs H.
Below and opposite: Under the loose canopy of the silk trees *Albizia julibrissin* (below), there is enough light for asters *Asteromoea mongolica* and fountain grass *Pennisetum alopecuroides* to bloom.
Giant *Miscanthus* fringes the driveway (opposite right) and turn this often overlooked area into a really attractive part of the garden.
The often multi-stemmed black birches *Betula nigra* have grown into handsome trees in the last twenty years (opposite far right). Their curly bark provides year round interest, and they even allow enough light through for the sun-craving *Sedum*.

side like us, but over the stalk straight into the core, the guts of the apple. Wolfgang the bear, the lion, the plant… Oehme's imagination does sometimes show a carefree childishness. As we turn into the driveway, the presence of towering *Miscanthus* announces the work of the team from Washington. A slightly raised pond lies in front of the living room windows, herbaceous perennials and unusual trees divert attention from the long, low building with its gently pitched roof, the stereotypical American house. It sometimes seems that in his heart, every American wants to be a rancher. Now, after fifteen years, this average house has been subordinated to the above average vegetation, most of all in the back garden. Three black birches (*Betula nigra*) and a strange silk tree (*Albizia julibrissin*) tower over the house, throw shadows on the terrace, allowing flickers of light through to perennials and grasses. Here too is stonecrop, although less plump than elsewhere. 'Don't believe what the catalogues say,' Oehme comments. 'Lots of things grow in shade, differently I'll admit, but they grow.' Over the roof to the south a low wall of perennials and grasses separates the lawn and the tennis court from the planted area of the garden. A stand of upright reed grass *Calamagrostis acutiflora* 'Stricta' grows by the pool, sharply contrasted by the Adam's needle *Yucca filamentosa*, which lies in full sun, and throws out

dazzling gold-yellow fireworks from August onwards.

Garden of Mrs So.

Fireworks of a quite different kind greet us in the distance. Our journey continues westwards through Long Island, past vineyards and those endless lawns that one could never describe as meadows. A senseless waste of space and energy, in Oehme's opinion. We're heading straight for the towering forest of light that is New York, but pass by as fast as possible. We won't even stop for a look at the masterpiece of the greatest ever American landscape architect, Frederick Law Olmstead, who 150 years ago blasted rocks and planted a hundred thousand trees and a million bushes to create Central Park in Manhattan, the world's first 'People's Park'. Anything was possible in this land of unlimited opportunity. Olmstead used dynamite in the construction of private gardens too. In the hilly country in eastern Pennsylvania, for example, loud bangs were heard more than once. The story goes that a certain Jacob Nolde wanted a steeper slope on his land to ski on, and that Olmstead rearranged the landscape with explosives. Nowadays, the wealthy fly to Colorado for their skiing, but the present owner, Mrs So., is delighted that the mountain was moved. And so the house stands loftier still over the estate, with the meadow flowing down the slope from the

Garden of Mrs So.
A narrow, natural stone path leads to the swimming pool at the rear of the house, flanked by the red flowers of the Japanese knotweed *Fallopia japonica* 'Crimson Beauty', *Miscanthus* and white *Asteromoea mongolica*.

terrace, flanked on both sides by colourful herbaceous perennials and grasses. Mrs So. feels at home here. She is, incidentally, one of the many leading ladies of the American Dream. In 1979 she took the cookies she was baking in a garage to the bosses of a global coffee shop chain. They loved them, and took the young woman on as a supplier. She is now a millionaire. Some of her dollars went into an estate, at the heart of which is a castle-like building, with a driveway several hundred metres long, flanked by groups of perennials and grasses. In autumn, with everything around a monotonous green, they offer a wonderful palette of colours. 'This garden has not four seasons but six or seven,' Mrs So. says, thus approaching the number that Karl Foerster had in mind for his rock garden, and which he used as the title for a ground-breaking book. Oehme is delighted with such praise, but with a broad smile has the last word: 'Only seven? Twelve!' So, just what is this garden? A forest, turned into a garden by Jacob Nolde to remind him of his home in Westfalia, into which Olmstead cut islands of spacious lawn. Decades later Oehme enhanced these spaces with grasses, herbaceous perennials and trees. A tried and tested division of labour was put to work here: Oehme designed the plantings, and van Sweden directed work on the terraces, paths, steps and ponds – everything that falls under the heading 'hardscaping'. It's all beautifully balanced. Solid luxurious garden furniture stands on the extensive terrace, separated from the slope by low walls and groupings of plants. At the

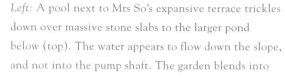

Garden of Mrs So.

Left: A pool next to Mrs So's expansive terrace trickles down over massive stone slabs to the larger pond below (top). The water appears to flow down the slope, and not into the pump shaft. The garden blends into the landscape on both sides of the slope with grasses and perennials (centre). *Miscanthus* and red knotweed *Bistorta amplexicaule* 'Firetail' (bottom) line another approach to the house.

Opposite: Miscanthus as undergrowth in the wood around the guest house.

sides of the incline grasses and perennials have grown into the summer view, while the lawn recedes into the distance. The fantastic view over the Pennsylvania hills dominates the picture, the plants enhancing rather than detracting from it. Flowerbeds and plants must therefore be neither too big nor too small, and although it is wonderful living in such a beautifully natural place, the hand of man should remain clearly visible too. Stone plays its part, but exactly situated and layered. There has to be water, but in a perfectly circular pool, from where it flows over heavy rock slabs to a natural pond at the edge of the slope. Perennials belong here too, some in carefully differentiated groupings and others, where

appropriate, merging together. This is the case under the trees for example. At the start of the construction process, Oehme thinned out the forest only when Mrs So. wasn't at home. Had it been up to her, he would never have been able to achieve the light conditions needed for his choice of plants. We wander through the garden, past the pool, down to the tennis court. But where has Wolfgang got to? We find him at the edge of the forest, collecting seeds which he stuffs into his bulging jute bag ahead of the trip to Virginia. These wingnut (*Pterocarya fraxinifolia*) seeds, originally from the Caucasus, will be just right for Virginia too, with Wolfgang as the catalyst.

Garden of Mr and Mrs Sh.

Opposite: The view from the house takes in the swimming pool and the dense barrier of various *Miscanthus* that hides the tennis court (top left).

Bare rock is a common feature (centre). *Miscanthus*, *Geranium* and *Stachys* all cope well with the conditions and are perfect for such natural designs.

Lavish fields of *Pennisetum* lead towards the paddocks that form part of the estate (bottom). Smaller trees like *Betula nigra* act as structural elements.

The tall perennials and grasses have not yet started to grow in spring, so Oehme planted hundreds of thousands of narcissus bulbs in the rocky ground (top right).

Garden of Mr and Mrs Sh.

Leaving Olmstead's landscapes, heading southwest through towns like Knauers and Manheim, we pass through Lancaster County, deep in mourning. Just a few days before, five students from the deeply religious Amish community, originally from Germany and the German speaking part of Switzerland, were shot dead at their school by a psychopath. The gloomy mood in our car is not lifted by the lack of new ideas for gun control, as reported on the radio. As we cross the wild Susquehanna river our mood lifts and the unrestrained nature all around calms and diverts us. Every cloud has a silver lining, the thought gives us hope. We pass by East Berlin, and our thoughts digress. The wooded Appalachians rise up ahead – the Blue Ridge Mountains, which from a distance really do seem to be covered by a blue veil, the result of a substance exuded by the pines. Between us and the mountains are fields, meadows and woods, punctuated by mostly old towns, such as Berryville, Virginia. We're expected at Mr and Mrs Sh's garden nearby. Mrs Sh. doesn't want 'fancy drawings', but insists on a visit from Wolfgang, with his on-the-spot expertise and his immaculate sense of proportion, spacing and groupings. The garden is a constant work in progress, but it never turns out as planned. Late last autumn, Oehme and his constant companion Carol Oppenheimer drilled holes in the stony, frozen soil and planted hundreds of thousands of bulbs. In the spring splashes of yellow narcissi light up the ground between the numerous limestone rocks that litter the landscape. In autumn the flame-coloured grasses brighten the thinned out woods, the *Miscanthus* under the tall trees have smaller seed heads and lack the heavy stems they would otherwise have in the open. The filigree growth is charming nonetheless. Oehme started by planting the tennis court area with *Miscanthus* and *Molinia*, and not with trees, as is the standard. The grasses paint their autumn colours of brown, yellow and beige in every conceivable shade, to which *Aster tataricus* adds a contrasting deep violet. It would be easy to get lost here among the grasses. From the house Mrs Sh. has a view over wide lawns – even OvS can't get away without these on estates like hers. But the lawn is merely a frame for the view of the rectangular swimming pool with its reddish dogwood, behind which a fantastic backdrop of waving grasses and perennials rises up from the summer onwards. What Oehme hinted at in the car has been dramatically realised here: the art of gardening has been introduced to nature and to a man-made landscape of horse paddocks, but in a way that only enriches. Nothing is taken from

At the foot of the Appalachians a magnificent drama plays out for weeks at a time, in the second half of the year. The flowers and fronds of the *Miscanthus sinensis* and *Pennisetum alopecuroides* catch the sun, matching the colours in the background.

the landscape. A massed planting of trees and perennials at the edge of the property is the next phase, to block out the view of her neighbour, who lives not 5 or 15 or 50 metres away, but at least 500. After all, this is America.

Garden of Mr and Mrs R.

Mr and Mrs R. don't have this problem. We reach their garden having followed the Appalachians for at least 100 kilometres. Also set in the midst of horse paddocks, the view from here is spectacular. The mountains rise to over 2,000 metres, and as one of the oldest ranges on earth is gently rounded and heavily wooded. As in Oehme and van Sweden's other gardens, water plays a significant role here, with a round swimming pool perfectly sited between house and paddocks. A wall, built on the principles of the English ha-ha, prevents the horses getting into the garden, and avoids the need for visible barriers, helping the garden blend into the landscape. The pool is also a mirror, reflecting the sky or the *Miscanthus* and *Pennisetum*, depending on your viewpoint. Even though walls, terraces, steps and a pergola are visible, we are constantly reminded of the designer's intention: the garden must not compete with nature, but rather support her. With their gardens, Oehme and van Sweden clear a path to nature, or at least to the memory of an experience of nature. But the differences are clear too. Their gardens have strong, clearly marked edges, and none of the mixed, random patterns of nature. The garden flows into the landscape, and with its generous proportions it tries to come closer to the grand dimensions of forest, meadow, river and hill. We are reminded of the great Pückler, who advised us to include in our designs 'every object of even remote interest that we as it were possess, however distant it may be.' This is of limited use in small city gardens, but in the country can be used to full effect, and proves wise advice. The Appalachians belong to the whole visual experience of the garden.

Opposite: Oehme doesn't always work on a lavish scale. Here, a smaller bed of reed grass *Calamagrostis* x *acutiflora* 'Stricta' draws attention to itself by the swimming pool.

Right: The enclosure of the vegetable garden needed a very delicate approach to ensure it stood out from the surrounding natural plantings.

Garden of Mr G.

We're staying in the country, even though we're leaving Virginia. Heading northwest, we bypass Washington and aim for Maryland's Eastern Shore, which is home to many of Oehme and van Sweden's gardens. This strip of land along the jumble of waterways in Chesapeake Bay, with a shore line that has probably never been accurately measured, is immensely popular for homes and weekend houses. It is punctuated by countless tiny bays created by the myriad rivers and streams that flow into Chesapeake Bay itself. Over 400 kilometres long, from the mouth of its main river, the Susquehanna, to the sea at Norfolk, Virginia, the 100,000 square kilometre area is fed by these many rivers and streams. Washington, Baltimore and Annapolis alone have more than enough wealthy folk who own homes on the bay, or would like to own one. Many plots have already been sold, and the shore reserved with a jetty. In summer temperatures can reach 40 degrees centigrade with 90 percent humidity and vast swarms of gnats. 'It's just like hell here in August, it's like an oven with mosquitoes in it,' is how one hardened local describes it. Even Wolfgang, just as hardy, has to take a break at lunchtime in October. Even so, city folk drive for two hours or more to reach their idyll, which is becoming ever more polluted by the urbanisation they are trying to get away from. But before we take the Bay Bridge to the Eastern Eastern Shore, we stop in the small town of Harwood. Many years ago Mr G. bought himself 7 hectares and 200 metres of shoreline and built a large weekend house. His swimming pool, beautifully set in a spacious wooden deck, has been seen in more than a few lifestyle magazines – pool in the foreground, Chesapeake Bay behind. In these photos there is always something that stands out like an exclamation mark. In typical OvS style, the garden as a whole has grasses and herbaceous perennials grouped

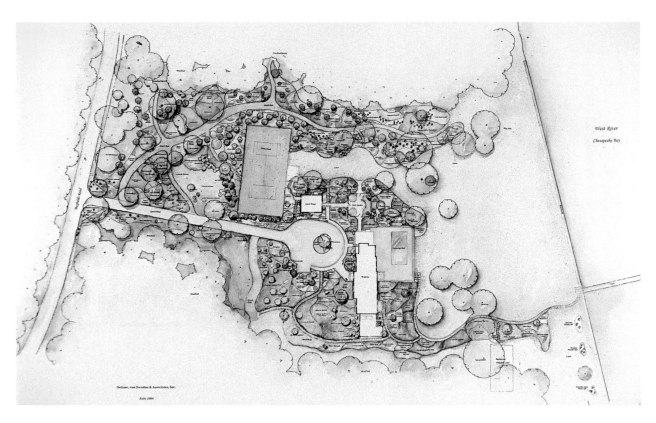

freely around trees and bushes, but this exclamation mark near the decking stands almost isolated from the rest. We are talking about an arrangement of *Calamagrostis*, which Oehme has situated on the north side of the deck. *Calamagrostis* x *acutiflora* 'Stricta', the same grass his cousin sent him from Denmark forty years ago, appears either as a rigid line or as a tight, unbroken bundle, depending on where you are standing, and can be seen from many parts of the house and garden. As it sprouts early and lasts until the first snows of winter this arrangement provides great value and is in the perfect location. Describing only one feature doesn't do the garden justice, and just for once let's talk numbers to convey the size of the place: Oehme planted 5,000 *Lysimachia clethroides*, 5,000 *Rudbeckia fulgida* 'Goldsturm', 500 *Hosta siedoldiana*, and 1,000 *Pennisetum alopecuroides*, to name just four of over forty plants he used. There are 100 *Miscanthus sinensis* 'Malepartus' alone, the cultivar introduced by Ernst Pagels, with its superb reddish flowers. Mr G. wanted nothing less than the impression of nature running things, with the visible hand of the designer fading as soon as possible. The dense plantings brought this about after just one year. A *New York Times* article in 1993 called it 'Instant Gardens with a Wild Look'. 'None of my guests has ever said anything about the exquisite design. Nature seems to have won,' says Mr

G., and sees 'the time I spend in the garden as a deep, almost religious experience. This garden has truly brought so much pleasure into my life.' This is balm to Oehme's soul; this recognition allows one of his many dreams to be fulfilled. Now well over eighty, Mr G. is back in contact. He's bought a new plot of land – let the planting begin!

Garden of Mrs S.

Looking east over the still waters of Chesapeake Bay, here over 20 kilometres wide, we can only guess at the two gardens on the other side. We leave in the early dawn to beat the traffic over the Bay Bridge. Where does this daily avalanche of metal go, how long will Americans go on commuting 100 kilometres every day, between the office and their new house in the suburbs? When the four-lane bridge between the Washington/ Baltimore conurbation and the sparsely populated Eastern Shore became too small, they just built another, with six lanes, 100 metres away. And they are already talking about a third bridge. America has galloped ahead of itself, and gallops on, blinkered, without knowing where. Even Wolfgang Oehme gets caught in jams, although less often now – he arranges his visits to miss the traffic, if at all possible. Somewhere, on a lonely spit of land at the mouth of the Choptank River, Mrs S. has realised her dream. Not one building, but several, as guests like to have their own house here. As the end of October approaches, we are reminded again of Foerster, speaking about fading and dying, about 'the impoverishment and theft of eternal riches. November sets forth a feast for the eyes. It's as if the host has turned off the lights after the party, and is sitting with a few friends enjoying a last drink in the twilight.' And so it is. Brown, beige and pale green dominate the view, as we enter the garden on a path of crushed shells. The all too rarely used *Rudbeckia maxima* is particularly effective, growing to head hight, but not so dense that it cannot still be used at the front of flowerbeds. The important thing is the grey-blue foliage below, and then in autumn the seed heads, almost black

Garden of Mr G.

Opposite top: The design for Mr G's garden shows the scale on which Oehme and van Sweden often have to work. Thousands of plants surround the geometric shapes of drive, house, guest house, terrace and tennis court.

Opposite below: The view from the shore of Chesapeake Bay comes to rest on the concentrated field of *Calamagrostis*, topped by *Miscanthus* that catch the last rays of the autumn sun.

against their beige stems. Mrs S. has her pool in front of the building, framed by high grasses and perennials, with a rustic fence visible every so often. The house was built as close to the water as possible, leaving no room at the back for the swimming pool and its attendant facilities. A wooden deck on stilts leads around the house, and in front of us is Chesapeake Bay. In one of the purest forms of landscape – the swamps and marshlands between two deep estuaries – Oehme and van Sweden have proved that their designs follow only one law – nature. From the living room you step onto the decking. Between there and the sea is a barrier made of just a few plants, not particularly colourful, about a metre tall, and just a little higher than the terrace. No railing is needed as the

plants act as the buffer for the lower lying area. Oehme looks at this garden, and sums up his entire philosophy and life's work: 'James and I haven't done much, we've really just simplified. We merely use a few plant varieties, but hundreds or thousands of each, which keep each other in check.' When it's windy here, which it almost always is, the garden is one waving mass, a sea of stems blowing freely in the breeze, not a path to be seen. But how else would one get from the deck to the water? The unsuspecting visitor doesn't see the narrow paths, created simply by not planting. Bark chips mark them out, nothing more. As they run virtually parallel to the terrace, they can't be seen from there or from the strip of lawn that runs between house and waterline. Simple. Brilliant.

Garden of Mrs S.

Opposite: Planting the margins of coastal gardens with plants like switchgrass *Panicum virgatum* 'Cloud Nine' is the best way to blend them into the landscape, matching the native vegetation.

Top right: With too little space between the bay and the houses, Oehme and van Sweden placed the pool inland, again using grasses and perennials to create a natural atmosphere.

Centre right: Barely noticeable, the paths between terrace and bay wind through swathes of perennials formed of just a few individual varieties.

Below right: The paths of crushed shells with natural stone slabs from the entrance and to the swimming pool match the coastal location.

Garden of Mr O'B.

Top left: The group of houses on Chesapeake Bay, along with the OvS garden, was given away in a lottery. The location right by the water inspired the designers to create a reed-like planting of *Miscanthus* and *Panicum*.

Below left: The second half of the year brings a riot of shapes and colours to the gardens of Oehme and van Sweden. Along the windy coast, the tall interwoven grasses paint an almost musical moving picture, masking the straight lines of the architecture.

Opposite: Just here Chesapeake Bay widens, resembling the ocean. From high summer onwards you dive into the sea of head-high grasses between terrace and shoreline. Two wooden chairs are all that's needed for an unforgettable spot.

Garden of Mr O'B.

A group of neighbouring white houses behind grasses and reeds attract our attention. This estate also comes courtesy of Mrs S., as well as OvS. Over 11 million people were interested in this house and garden, but only one would get it. 'The gardens of Oehme and van Sweden cost a fortune. But you can boast about them. An OvS is a Ferrari amongst gardens,' wrote the columnist Duncan Spencer in 1997 in *Capital Style*. It's very rare to be given a Ferrari as a present – but this one really was free. A TV station put house and garden up as a give-away in 2002, probably to boost their viewing figures. The new owner would have been welcomed by the *Miscanthus*, and escorted along the driveway, just as we are now.

Because of its proximity to the bay, this house is also on stilts. Standing on the terrace, the garden lies at our feet, grasses and perennials flowing together, *Amsonia hubrichtii* between solo *Miscanthus* throughout, next to fields of violet *Aster oblongifolius* 'October Skies'. There's no lawn between terrace and sea here, just a path through a thicket of *Panicum virgatum* 'Cloud Nine'. This path ends at the narrow strip of sand the sea has carved out. But this spot wouldn't be half as good without the two weather-beaten garden chairs. And so we sit, one left, one right, the rustling switchgrass behind us, the sand beneath us, the sky above us, and the sea before us. This place, this moment – unforgettable. We can take the path back to the buildings round to the right, over mown

grass in which, thanks to climate change, early season *Miscanthus* has self-sown. On one side the path takes us back to the entrance through a field of *Miscanthus* and *Pennisetum*, whilst on the other we pass the rectangular swimming pool, behind which is a spectacular setting of autumn colour. It's hard to separate the wilderness behind the garden from the symphony of grasses and perennials – it's all as one. On the raised terrace the talk is of 'perfecting nature'. If that were at all possible it has happened here, at least as far as our aesthetic sense is concerned. Yes, we would do well to embrace the many nuances of beige and brown as primary garden colours, merging into grey and black, gold and silver. Not to appreciate the pale yellow *Miscanthus* stems and

the light brown *Rudbeckia maxima*, and to wield the secateurs in November or even earlier, is to cut off not only an inspiring decoration but also a whole season.

Garden of Family B.

'Spring is easy,' Wolfgang comments as we get into the car. We know just what he means. It's the same for us, our gardens also at their best at that time of year. After that we're in for a bumpy ride as they threaten to come off the rails. A structure of box or yew, a rose arch or some other ornamentation often has to come to the rescue. We've now seen a number of gardens built by Oehme and van Sweden and not missed the lack of formal classical elements. Their gardens, described some time ago as

Top left: During October the delicate *Amsonia hubrichtii* changes to warm browns, and combines wonderfully with the low growing *Aster oblongifolius*. The blocks of colour vanish into seeming infinity through layers of grasses and perennials.

Below left: Grasses such as *Pennisetum* and *Panicum* have faded from green to beige and form a perfect bridge between garden and nature. The view from the pool rises step by step to a backdrop of wild and cultivated plants.

Opposite top left: A magnificent stand of old oaks brings half-shade, alongside wider open areas, where *Bistorta amplexicaule* and the attractive goldenrod *Solidago rugosa* 'Fireworks' flourish and add autumn colour. The *Miscanthus* in the background gets more light, its fronds catching the sun.

Opposite top right: Accompanied by *Panicum* and *Miscanthus*, this slender path leads from the wood to the lawn by the bay. The tall plant on the right of the picture, similar to *Miscanthus*, is the rarer plume grass *Saccharum ravennae*.

Opposite below left: While the grasses are waiting to sprout in early spring, a mass of narcissi enliven the scene. The building in the background is the main house on the estate.

Opposite below right: The perfectly round swimming pool lies, slightly raised, at the top of the slope down to the bay. From the perspective of the swimmer, the water in the pool merges seamlessly with the water in the bay beyond, the lawn becoming invisible.

the 'New American Landscape', show a remarkably light touch, just as many great paintings do at first sight. In 1997 Family B. bought a large house with various outbuildings on a peninsula not far from the give-away house. Here, the meadows and woods are surrounded on three sides by the placid waters of a small bay. A modest entrance of bollards topped with bird sculptures, and three eye catching *Lagerstroemia* trees, lead us into the garden. The driveway curves towards the house, bordered in spring by thousands of narcissi, and later by *Pennisetum*, *Miscanthus*, *Panicum* and *Solidago* 'Fireworks', a more delicate goldenrod cultivar than usually found in

these parts. *Hosta* 'Sum and Substance' with its enormous leaves, thrives under the trees. It is reminiscent of an English country park, with old trees dotted around a recently cut meadow. Oehme and van Sweden have only left their traces at the very edges, by the paths, at the entrance, on the veranda and terrace, by the perfectly circular swimming pool, and down at the waterline. Towering *Miscanthus* dominate the banks, perfect for this environment, conspicuous but harmoniously linking the garden to the shore. To bring a little more life to this world of muted colours the family has also dotted some eye-catching furniture around the meadows.

Garden of Mr K.

We now head northwards. Alternating woods and farmland are cut through by wide roads and split by sprawling crossroads with all the blessings of American civilisation – gas stations, supermarkets, fast food outlets, poodle parlours. At one of these crossroads our vegetarian hero has spotted a health food shop serving hot food. Lunch beckons. Wolfgang is a particularly attentive passenger, spotting healthy food from miles away, and he never misses one of 'his' plants or some interesting herb by the roadside. If we're lucky he might even tell us something useful about it. Cultivated plants, on the

other hand, get about as much attention as a hamburger stand. That's what happens to a vast white, pink and red field of *Cosmos bippinatus* (cosmos or Mexican aster). The thousands of blooms make a spectacular display, but Oehme dismisses it as just so much agriculture, and we race on by. We pass through pretty Chestertown to answer the call of another Chesapeake Bay garden. Haven't we seen it all before? Not really; even though the palette of colours and plants may be limited, it's the location and on-the-spot conditions that differentiate one garden from another. Sometimes nature has prepared the ground herself, at others it's all the work of the designer. Mr K's slightly elevated garden stretches away into a landscape of fields, small woods and swamp.

The main garden and terrace lie to the west, where great swathes of *Perovskia atriplicifolia* (Russian sage) and *Pennisetum* conceal the wall that absorbs the drop from the terrace to the surrounding land. Not one tree comes into view, just a low growing *Lagerstroemia* next to the round pond on the deck. Everything is on a large scale – buildings, garden, and landscape. Oehme could let his leitmotif run free here – think big. Even before the house was built Oehme and van Sweden laid down a pond and surrounded it with 30,000 plants, 2,000 *Miscanthus* alone, plus thousands of *Panicum* switch grass and *Solidago* goldenrod. It's hard to say where the garden ends and nature begins. Stalking through the *Miscanthus* jungle is an unforgettable experience, above us just a

Garden of Mr K.

Opposite: Even before the house was built, Wolfgang Oehme and James van Sweden created a small lake surrounded with plants. Wolfgang, along with a few gardeners, planted 2,000 *Miscanthus* alone.

Top right: The metre wide path around the lake leads through a head-high *Miscanthus* jungle, relieved now and then by birch or alder. The plants here find the high water table very congenial.

Below right: A small water lily pond has been sunk into the terrace, facing the bay, partly shaded by the diminutive crape myrtle *Lagerstroemia indica*.
The embankment running down to the lawn is mostly planted with *Pennisetum alopecuroides*.

steel-blue sky and gently waving silver-beige fronds. One of the garden's highlights, at least for the owner, is the walled garden, where Oehme's influence cannot be seen. The wall alone, isolating and restricting, is an alien form to him. There is a greater variety of plants too, and a red East Asian style pavilion at one end, with a bright half open wooden summerhouse at the other. Maybe the owner feels a bit lost in his wide open spaces after all, and is looking for the formal enclosures and classical forms from garden history – a bit of the Far East here and romantic England there. Next to the pavilion is a pine, *Pinus contorta contorta*, which was tended in a nursery for over thirty years before finding a new home here, at a price that ran to six figures. The hot climate and hard clay soil

form a complicated alliance that gives even Wolfgang Oehme headaches. The battle of the pine is not yet over.

Garden of Mr and Mrs v.D.

A short walk away, up a gentle slope, lies another garden. Wolfgang Oehme is laying out some newly delivered plants, and our companion Carol Oppenheimer comes along to Mr and Mrs v.D's weekend house too. Carol thought she knew a bit about ornamental grasses until she met Wolfgang. James Buckler, Director of the Horticulture Office at the world famous Smithsonian Institute, admitted many years ago after an Oehme lecture, 'this man probably knows more about plants than any other landscape designer in this country.' Carol

Oppenheimer thought so too. At a chance meeting many years ago she asked Oehme about his working methods, and he asked her to accompany him. No sooner said than done. For years Oppenheimer was permitted to watch and to weed. Rewarded only with food and knowledge, she has learned her trade and is now allowed to create her own plant designs. Carol is happy with this as time spent in Oehme's gardens is a delight. As is the walk through the v.D's garden, which also features a somewhat out-of-the-way pond, dominated by *Panicum virgatum* 'Cloud Nine' in vast masses. But with all this water around us, why do we need another pond? Simple. Water is a superb medium to create the perfect effect with grasses. We've seen this at Mr K's and here too. The comparatively delicate building, raised on stilts, stands in the middle of the garden and is reached by a drive that typically

Garden of Mr K.
Above: View over the lake to the house. On the opposite bank is a sea of shimmering goldenrod *Solidago rugosa* 'Fireworks', planted by the thousand, with an adjacent grouping of *Miscanthus*. To achieve the desired effects of colour and form in this wide open flat landscape vast numbers of plants are needed.

Garden of Mr and Mrs v. D.
Opposite: Oehme and van Sweden have created another garden right next door. As house and garden are much smaller far fewer plants are needed, but being set in the same landscape, the selection is very similar.

winds around a thickly planted island. One of the countless arms of the Chesapeake Bay can be glimpsed behind a stand of old trees. This really is a dream house by the sea – built of wood, with a wooden terrace, and a wooden walkway leading through ornamental grasses to the landing stage, where the weekend sailor has already prepared the next fishing tour. Ospreys circle over the bay and vultures over the land, cormorants swoop low along the shore line, crickets make the only sound apart from the water lapping on the rocks and pushing driftwood onto the small beach. Mighty clumps of *Miscanthus*, *Pennisetum* and *Molinia* separate land from water with a real sense of exhilaration. Between the house and the bay, sculpture-like stands of *Miscanthus* appear out of large areas of *Pennisetum* and *Euphorbia palustris*. Everything is in constant motion. A great

sugar maple spreads its crown over all, creating varied light conditions beneath. Knowing the ingredients is part of it, a journalist once wrote about Oehme and van Sweden's art, the rest is knowing how to turn them into a splendid feast. Oehme had occasionally smuggled a new plant into the garden of Mrs v.D. without her knowledge, from heaven alone knows where and in one of his many pockets. She penned a tribute to 'her secret gardener' on the occasion of his seventy-fifth birthday. 'Wolfgang, you are welcome in my garden at any time, day or night.' The last three words were said with a wink: she knows that even after dark Wolfgang is out and about, making sure that everything is in order.

Garden of Mr and Mrs O.

Dusk is upon us, our work in the flatlands of the Eastern

Shore is done, and we turn our backs on the gardens by the bay. Our destination this time is the hill country north of Baltimore, Mr and Mrs O's garden. This is farming country – white grain silos, Friesian cows in the fields and rusting, oversized cars behind the houses. With classical music surging in the background, the conversation still revolves around Mr K's garden and the need to replace plants that are struggling in those conditions with plants that can cope better. Even Wolfgang Oehme is not omnipotent and learns from his

mistakes. They will review the situation next year, and maybe Mr K. will have to dig deep in his pockets again. But if you can afford 2,000 *Miscanthus* you won't baulk at replacing thirty *Molinia* with some sedges. Oehme and van Sweden have discovered that the more you spend on your garden, the more likely you are to look after it. Here in Mrs O's garden in northern Maryland everything is just fine. Now over twenty years old, the design and the plants are well established. It all started with English style borders, but they were much too labour intensive.

Garden of Mr and Mrs v. D.

Opposite: Hundreds of *Panicum virgatum* 'Cloud Nine' growing on an island in the lake. On the opposite bank *Aster oblongifolius* 'October Skies' adds some robust colour to the browns of autumn.

Top right: The red seedheads of individually planted shrubs bring colour to the autumn, but can hardly out do the *Miscanthus* fronds waving in the wind.

Centre right: A broad band of goldenrod *Solidago rugosa* 'Fireworks' completes the planting near the house. This beautiful variety is more delicate and has longer panicles than other types.

Below right: The wooden walkway continuing up to the elevated entrance through the garden between grasses and the spreading marsh spurge *Euphorbia palustris*.

Garden of Mr and Mrs O.
The highlights of this garden in the Maryland hills just before
the onset of winter are *Miscanthus sinensis* 'Purpurascens' in the
foreground, *Pennisetum alopecuroides* and *Calamagrostis* x *acutiflora*
'Karl Foerster' in front of and behind the swimming pool.

Now wide beds surround the pool and lawn with typical herbaceous perennials, grasses and the occasional small tree. *Sedum* 'Autumn Joy', *Perovskia*, day lilies or *Rudbeckia* 'Goldsturm' form elongated groups and combine harmoniously with the varied grasses between the fields and woods, but at the same time create a tension with the ubiquitous landscape, which they do not wish to block out.

Garden of Mr and Mrs Bu.

The route to our last garden takes us southwards towards Baltimore, over and between the hills. The closer we get to the city, the more farmland is being swallowed up by generic dream homes. The lightweight houses are put together rapidly using traditional methods. Today's wooden frameworks will be panelled, fitted out and occupied in a matter of weeks. Fleets of lawnmowers are

Garden of Mr and Mrs O.

Top left: Russian sage *Perovskia atriplicifolia* brings an unusually cool note into this garden in autumn, providing a striking contrast with the warm tones of stonecrop *Sedum telephium* 'Autumn Joy'.

Top right: The garden is not meant to be cut off from the agricultural landscape, but merely fenced clearly in. Hence the grasses and perennials are often almost transparent and the tree tops start at eye level.

Below: The warmer colours of *Miscanthus*, *Sedum* and *Begonia grandis* are particularly valuable in the cooler days of late October.

replacing tractors in this 'land without nightingales', as the poet Leonard Lenau satirically described the US in the nineteenth century. For him, the distinctive practicality of the Americans had gone too far, and the poetry of the wild, the love of the precious heart of life was already falling victim to rationalisation and mechanisation. But alongside these flat pack developments there are also individual new houses. Hardly visible from the street, only accessible with the right access code, the heavy wooden gates open and admit us to a road which takes us up hill and down. A farm on the opposite side of the valley gives the impression that all is well with the world. We are not particularly welcome in this private, walled-in world, even Wolfgang Oehme is a stranger. A lavish Japanese garden has been created here, certainly very tasteful, but we have come to expect something quite different from one of Oehme's projects. So we don't linger here, but head down into the wooded valley where Mrs Bu. has her studio and Mr Bu. his private motor museum. The studio garden is still dominated by influences from the Far East, with just a few, mostly evergreen, plants, a Buddha and a simple stone column. It's the same question that Oehme always asks himself: 'In this wonderful natural place what am I supposed to change? What can I as a garden designer do without diluting the mood and still if possible enhance people's pleasure? You have to restrain yourself,' is one of the short answers you get if you ask Oehme to sum up his philosophy in one sentence. James van Sweden expanded on this in an interview: 'No-one can do what we can. Because now no-one can restrain themselves in this giant supermarket like we can.' Restraint becomes a virtue in this land of excess, a virtue which is otherwise on the endangered list. Restraint is also the watchword for the garden by the museum, a grey windowless box. Trees have been cleared for the car park. Plane trees stand on either side, underplanted with *Calamagrostis* and *Helianthus angustifolius* 'Gold Lace'. Even with their bright yellow flowers, the colour scheme here in the woods is not too garish. Under lofty oaks and maples, in neat rows or in groupings that seem to merge (depending on your viewpoint), grow *Panicum virgatum*, *Pycnanthemum muticum*, *Amsonia hubrichtii* and *Senecio aureus*. Restraint – a term, and an approach to design that is ever present on our garden journey. Back at the car, Wolfgang hands out kiwifruit. He eats his, skin and all, gaining maximum benefit from all the vitamins, and smiles at our surprise. For dessert he picks a handful of weeds, which he polishes off right down to the earthy roots. Still chewing, he gets back in the car, chuckling happily. Another good day. Oehme's like a puppy, tugging constantly at his lead and following only his own nose, but a day with him is never boring. As evening arrives we turn into Joppa Road. We're in Towson, one of Baltimore's satellite towns. We come to a halt in the driveway of number 511 A. The vegetation is rampant, dead wood lies around everywhere, and stones are piled up here and there. This is Wolfgang's home.

Garden of Mr and Mrs Bu.

Above: The gardening year is almost over, most plants have faded, some still have seeds, and a few are still in flower, like the sunflower *Helianthus angustifolius* 'Gold Lace'.

Top and centre right: In the woods near house and car museum stands the studio, whose garden was designed in a Far Eastern style at the artist's request. Ground cover is provided by the shade loving dwarf mondo grass *Ophiopogon japonicus* 'Nana'.

Below right: In the sparse woods near the museum, a beautiful front to back formation of *Senecio aureus, Amsonia hubrichtii, Pycnanthemum muticum* and *Panicum virgatum*.

Opposite: The reliance on just a few plants works well around the museum's car park. Late flowering *Helianthus* and already faded *Calamagrostis* grow under the plane trees.

Heaven under the clouds
Oehme's garden in Towson, Maryland

Wolfgang Oehme can't be described as religious in the conventional sense. For him, heaven is on earth. To be more specific, he points to a spot on the map about 30 kilometres north of Baltimore – Towson. Not a particularly pretty town, built in the American way, an uncomfortable sort of heaven. Had he been even more precise his finger would have picked out 511 A West Joppa Road, where he bought a house in 1988, and started his own garden. Joppa, the biblical Jaffa and now part of Tel Aviv, is where oranges grow higher then elsewhere. No oranges grow in Oehme's Joppa, but many of his favourites do soar skywards: *Persicaria polymorpha*, for example, long-flowering, upright, compact, which Oehme persistently sent to every corner of the globe and

Left: When Wolfgang Oehme bought his current house, the garden was mainly rectangular lawn on a gentle slope. The two-storey house remained much as it was, with its raised decking, but the lawn totally vanished. In the picture below, taken twenty years later from the same viewpoint, the house has almost disappeared.

Opposite: The plans show about two thirds of the back garden. Oehme created a dynamic cascade with the open areas, lily pond and swimming pool, doing away with the gentle incline.

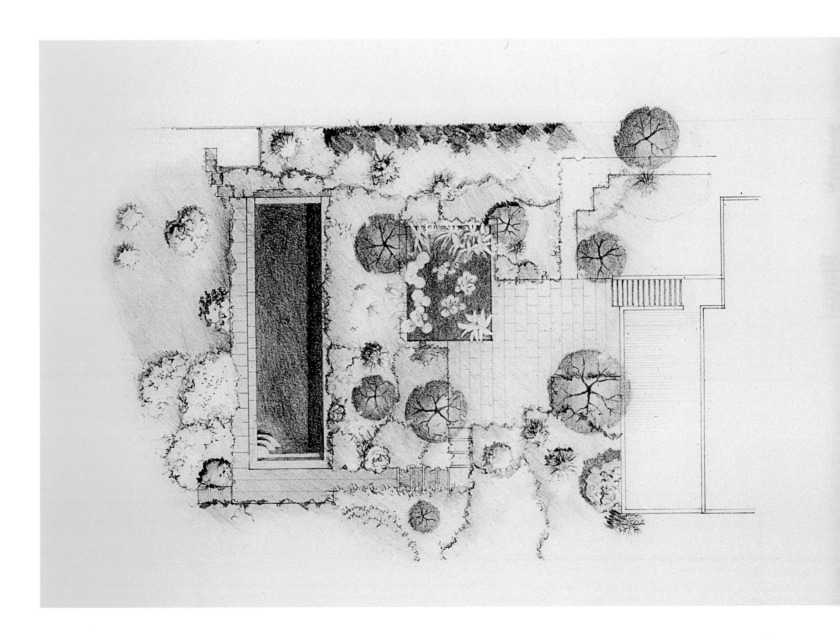

Oehme's garden in Towson, Maryland 87

is now a regular in nursery catalogues. And of course many of the plants he uses in his clients' gardens are also in his. But the choice is so great and his garden so small that individual plants have to be planted in smaller numbers. The wonderful composition of the garden can be seen when Wolfgang and his son Roland have cut back the perennials and grasses in early spring. It's amazing what can be done with a rectangular lawn that until 1988 fell evenly away to the bottom of the slope. Oblong slabs – as always Pennsylvania Bluestone – form the path and terrace, enclose the water lily pond and, lower down, the swimming pool, all vital horizontal surfaces in the design of the slope. Between the pools and along the fences there is plenty of room for his plants, competing for space and light in summer, growing over

edges and borders, becoming an absolute jungle. *Inula racemosa*, *Aster tataricus*, and *Miscanthus sinensis* all tower over Oehme and his guests. Plants heavy with dew and rainwater hang over the only path that leads down to the vegetable garden. Getting wet is an unavoidable part of life here. Most of the work in the garden, cutting back and mulching, is done by the end of winter. There is no lawn, and as soon as the perennials start to grow, weeds don't stand a chance.

Like most gardeners, Wolfgang Oehme is never totally happy, but when visitors arrive he is visibly proud of himself – and needs to talk. This was certainly the experience of Klaus-Jürgen Evert, a landscape architect from Stuttgart. He arrived at dusk, and after a bite to eat was looking forward to a good night's sleep to get

over his jetlag. But Oehme would have none of it. His torchlight guided tour of the garden, plant by plant, lasted until 1 a.m.

Those who are neat and tidy will not feel particularly comfortable in his garden. 'It's a wild thing in the early fall,' wrote Beth Smith in 1996 in *Garden Style*. More than ten years later, like its owner, it has aged a bit, but has remained wild. Still pretty fit, one might say, but going a touch thin on top. The odd tree here and there has died, but Oehme lets them lie for a while, providing food and shelter for a variety of animals and fungi. One thing lives off another – to tidy all this up would be to break the cycle. In this wilderness of leaves of various shapes and sizes, the terrace and swimming pool form a precise structural component. While the water lily pond

Above: In autumn, the lofty perennials, such as *Aster tataricus*, close in on the swimming pool and hide its straight edges. Oehme still likes to cool off between his favourite plants with a refreshing dip.

Opposite: Oehme only cuts the grasses and perennials back in late winter, and then mulches the plants with the cuttings. By May there is still an uninterrupted view of the two pools.

is totally overgrown, to the joy of the frogs that converse happily with Oehme, the pool (about 15 metres by 3.5 metres) is the only space in the whole garden totally free of plants. In 1998 the journalist Adrian Higgins wrote a daring analysis of the owner: 'The very idea of Wolfgang Oehme in swimming trunks is at best comical. With his goatee, thick-rimmed glasses and his accent a white coat would be more appropriate – the Professor wandering round his living laboratory, peering at a beloved plant for the thousandth time and still discovering something new about it.' Higgins would be disappointed; Oehme still swims here regularly, and he has never walked through his garden in a white coat like a pensive academic, just as a gardener, occasionally surprised by what he finds but mostly just getting on with the job at hand.

So these 2,000 square metres really do encompass an earthly paradise. While others look for their Creator in church or under candle-lit pine boughs on Christmas Eve, Wolfgang is here. Heaven knows, there's plenty to be found.

Left: Wolfgang Oehme collects things. He has decorated the wooden bollards along the driveway with stones he has found along the way, making the boundary markers of the wilderness hard to miss.

Opposite: Seldom to be found just sitting in his own garden, Oehme's overgrown wilderness (seen here from the first floor) has become a wildlife paradise amongst the manicured gardens of his neighbours.

Success with Wolfgang

James van Sweden: Thirty years' partnership with a plant freak

Above left: Wolfgang Oehme and James van Sweden often have a hand in building the gardens they design. This picture shows them in the mid-1970s unloading Oehme's Volkswagen in Washington DC.

Above right: By the end of the 80s they had moved to their current offices in Washington's Capitol Hill.

Life is really a series of coincidences, in between which we can take time to think and make our choices. If I had not continued my studies in Holland, the land of my fathers, I would not have encountered Professor Bijhouwer. His advice totally changed my life, without his ever knowing it. He recommended I get in touch with a gentleman called Wolfgang Oehme in Baltimore when I returned home to the US after my studies in 1964. Bijhouwer had met him at a conference in Switzerland in 1958. Our first meeting made a big impression on me. Wolfgang was sitting in his VW Variant, which was stuffed full of tools and plants. He designed gardens, and built them himself. Although I was working in a big town planners' office, we met repeatedly over the next few years and I started helping Wolfgang with his gardens. My desire to get involved, to get my hands dirty, to change the world became ever more urgent.

Then I bought a house in Washington, and in 1971 we created the garden together, fundamentally different to the usual American garden. Instead of a lawn and a few evergreen shrubs there was an energy and lushness that all my guests admired, and which gave me the idea that there must be a market for this style in the USA. We soon converted a bedroom into a small office, and built up a clientele of people who had seen the garden. Even after we went into formal partnership in 1975 our clients didn't have to spend their money on designs. They wanted a garden and they wanted people who didn't just design, but also got their hands dirty. This realisation became our strategy. We got our hands dirty, and still do, right in front of our clients. This is even more Wolfgang's element than mine. It sounds banal, but this is one of the main reasons for our success.

The other is that Wolfgang and I are totally different. He is a plantsman through and through, grounded in the soil, usually inward looking, reticent, a quiet soul. By contrast, I have to tell everyone what I'm doing and thinking of doing, to share my expectations and fantasies. It shouldn't really have worked, but the opposite happened. As individuals we are not geniuses, but the idea of working together was inspired. In the early 1980s a newspaper wrote about our partnership, that we had my extrovert charm to thank for clients swarming around us like bees round Wolfgang's flowers. And more: as partners each of us drove the other to perfection. We both planned and planted the gardens for our clients, but I was the front man who built up contacts, drank martinis with the right people and acted as PR agent. 'And Oehme is the botanical wunderkind.' Yes, this was the case: without my constant contact with newspapers, journals and important people we wouldn't have been half as famous or received nearly so many lucrative commissions. And without Wolfgang's unique talent for painting pictures with plants, I would never have been able to convince the media. These pictures remind us Americans of a lost landscape – the prairie. Without at all intending to, we

Opposite: Oehme and van Sweden had achieved star status in the garden design world by the mid-1990s. Publicity photos are taken mainly on-site.

Right: At the start of the century James built a holiday home on Chesapeake Bay. The same view today would show a natural stone path leading through countless grasses and perennials to the house.

successfully satisfy a yearning in our country. We create an image of what has been lost, right in front of your door.

So our success is really a combination of circumstances. One thing, it seems to me, is fundamental. Wolfgang and I were once asked for the definition of the garden. After due reflection, I wrote by way of an answer, 'a garden is a place where you can get your hands on nature. We can train our bodies and minds; with an active life in the garden you can even do without the help of a therapist.' In our gardens at least.

The prophet in his own land
A permanent commitment to Towson

You can be sure Wolfgang Oehme won't be late if you arrange to meet him at 7 a.m. He gets up early, and before our meeting has already been out and about for hours. He eats breakfast in the car – a couple of bananas, maybe an apple, pear or cucumber as well – and heads for various places in Towson, regardless of the weather, at dawn or dusk. These places include 'his' park next to the courthouse, 'his' median strips and roadsides in the centre of town, and 'his' garden at the Sheppard Pratt Hospital. They are like children, needing care in and attention. These children have never been officially his own, but for decades Wolfgang has been trying to change the face of his town, as quietly and unbureaucratically as

Above left: A view of a garden at the Sheppard Pratt Hospital in Towson. Oehme persists in using dead wood to help with the natural process of decay and growth – not to everyone's taste!

Below left: Patients and staff at the hospital see this garden as a real blessing. Here, a view in summer with the white *Persicaria polymorpha* and *Echinacea purpurea*.

Opposite: Oehme checks up on the garden he voluntarily designed sometimes twice a day. The narrow path winds between *Rosa* 'Knock Out' and *Panicum virgatum* 'North Wind'.

Whether the town library gardens, the garden in front of the Presbyterian Church or the median strips of its widest streets, Wolfgang Oehme has left his mark on his home town of Towson. On Charles Street he and his friends planted hundreds of Russian sage *Perovskia atriplicifolia* (above left), and on the four-lane Towsontown Boulevard, *Asteromoea mongolica* (below left) or tall *Miscanthus* underplanted with fields of perennials bloom from late summer (right).

possible. They should call it Wolfgangtown, he thinks, but that will never happen. Even though the town makes use of their internationally famous landscape architect, he remains a thorn in the side of the county authorities, constantly doing unpaid work and getting involved where he shouldn't. What sort of person goes out weeding the courthouse gardens by moonlight? And why would a healthy, sane man plant little red flags by the perennials and trees on the busy Towsontown Boulevard? These are actually to point out new plants he has planted to the municipal gardeners, in case they pull them up whilst weeding. There is a lot of superficial knowledge in America's green space maintenance teams.

Even though the courthouse gardens are Towson's only tourist attraction, drawing in visitors by the coachload from far and wide, the authorities still do not fully appreciate the achievements of their atypical gardening celebrity. 'Only painstaking persistence will make you healthy and happy,' wrote Karl Foerster. Taking this literally, Wolfgang Oehme doesn't miss an

opportunity to spread the news about the park, to offer private tuition to the county's gardeners and to advertise for weeding volunteers in the newspaper. Bill Vondrasek, Chief Horticulturist for Baltimore City, once helped out with a tour of the gardens. He remembers how little concern Oehme had for the needs of the visitors, thinking only of weeds and work to be done, and falling back on nature's own gifts: 'We toured the courthouse gardens on a Sunday afternoon, and no-one had eaten at all since breakfast. Passing a cherry tree laden with fruit, the first word I heard was "Lunch!" Ten minutes was all the time we had, then it was off to weed some astilbes.' Oehme even holds his birthday party at the courthouse, with guests bent double and clutching a hoe rather than a cake fork. In 1988 he transformed a flat space of lawn and flowers into a gently sculpted landscape with an astonishing variety of plants. 'We want to bring nature into town, we want a park that will change throughout the year,' he explained to local television reporters. Squirrels returned and even a fox was spotted. People spend their lunch

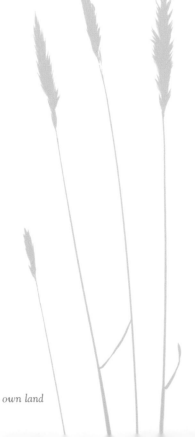

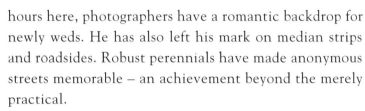

hours here, photographers have a romantic backdrop for newly weds. He has also left his mark on median strips and roadsides. Robust perennials have made anonymous streets memorable – an achievement beyond the merely practical.

He has most recently turned his attention to the grounds of the Sheppard Pratt Hospital, where with the help of Carol Oppenheimer and his son Roland, he has planted trees, grasses and perennials, and as in some of his other gardens the long lasting *Rosa* 'Knock Out'. Staff, patients and visitors use the 600 square metre eastern garden and the western courtyard garden, which was completed in 2007. Oehme comes here almost every day to weed, fill out his plantings, place old logs and fungi and bury banana skins as rose fertilizer. But not everyone understands the circle of life or just how many beneficial bacteria live in dead wood, and not everyone likes this sort of garden design. Some even try to tidy up. But Oehme stubbornly replaces the rotten branches, and ignores the dislike some feel for him. It's always been the same, whether in his sandpit, at school or at college; he's always been an odd character, and always utterly convinced that what he does is right. Why should old age change that?

Opposite: Twenty years ago Oehme started to redesign the flat lawns outside the courthouse. First the area was gently regraded and then thickly planted with herbaceous perennials.

Below: Miscanthus, Sedum and *Eupatorium maculatum* 'Gateway' are at their best in late summer. Oehme is constantly reminding the Council to leave the plants in situ until winter.

Right: In 1994 Wolfgang Oehme was inducted into the Towson Gardens Hall of Fame, honoured for his work on the new courthouse gardens. The variety of plants here is unusual for American parks, and it has become Towson's only tourist attraction. Even so, the fight against the pro-lawn faction on the Council goes on.

Opposite: The red blooms of *Miscanthus sinensis* 'Malepartus' combine beautifully with *Sedum telephium* in autumn. These and many other plants have made the gardens famous beyond the city limits, and have provided local workers with a place for lunch, all the residents with somewhere to recharge their batteries after work, and newly weds with a lovely backdrop for their photographs.

Awards continue to arrive, and Towson has honoured him twice for his voluntary work, first in 1989 and again in 1994. Baltimore County followed suit in 2003.

And tonight, after dark, Wolfgang will get back into his car. There's always a good reason to visit his children.

With pen and spade

The everyday life of a gardening landscape architect

At nearly eighty, you could call Wolfgang Oehme a sprightly pensioner. But this description, and all that it implies, doesn't fit with his everyday life. His daily routine is far from monotonous, and he is always busy gardening. Each day is filled as satisfyingly as the previous and the next. He doesn't like holidays unless they are somehow gardening related, Sundays and public holidays are just days when no-one is in the office and work on all his projects comes to a stop. But nature doesn't stand still, and there's always something to be done. 'Weed and eat' is his motto. In winter he changes it to 'read and eat', and not just because it rhymes. If there is no weeding to be done, he immerses himself in his library, reads *Spiegel* and the *Nordamerikanische Wochenpost* from cover to cover, which he rarely has time for from March to December. He's always on the lookout for interesting stories to pass on. Someone has calculated, he read recently, that America uses all the oil it imports from the Middle East just to power its lawnmowers. A scandal. One newspaper for German Americans has established that Karl May, the author of many books set in the American Wild West, is one of the most successful German writers of all time, which is music to Oehme's ears. Oehme thinks he is the most successful planter of herbaceous perennials of all time, and he could well be right. At any rate, his favourite tool is not the architect's pencil, but the gardener's narrow, lightweight spade. It's always in his car and he'll use it as a walking stick as time marches on.

He recently revealed, still full of energy, that not content with planting millions of grasses and perennials, he is setting his new target at billions. In this at least, Oehme is totally American. He thinks in terms of big spaces but short timeframes, and always looks to the future.

Those who work with Oehme must be ready for anything. He doesn't say much, and then only exactly what he wants and when he wants to. Thanks to his child-like innocence one minute, and his grandfatherly grumpiness the next, he remains so unpredictable that only very few succeed in telling him to behave himself. He'll wear his dark suit to attend an award ceremony, but will then wander off to do some weeding during the speeches. Most speakers, clients, friends and acquaintances prefer to let him be, and are grateful, in the end, to have known such an unusual man.

Oehme's so-called routine is varied. He spends little time at his Washington office, mainly reading his post, making appointments and immersing himself in his plans. His replies to colleagues are usually brief, leaving James van Sweden, Charles Turner and the three junior partners to run the business. Managing people and money is not really his thing. He is happiest outdoors. In his gardens he lays out perennials, grasses and shrubs to be planted by his landscape contractors, and at the nursery he casts a critical eye over the plants he needs for his clients, and his team digs up what he selects. He is always on the lookout for new plants. Sometimes he slips into the

role of a gardening Robin Hood, pocketing a handful of narcissus bulbs intended for one of his wealthy clients, and diverting them to the garden of someone who can't afford them. He is famously taciturn unless you ask him for advice, and then the words just burst forth. His lectures to students, garden clubs or professional associations are delivered in a quiet, halting murmur, which leaves some of his audience struggling to follow his words. His Saxon accent trails after him on these occasions, sometimes rendering even Latin, the lingua franca of the plant world, useless. His 'jumble of half learned English and forgotten German,' as Wolfgang Koeppen once described it, is often rescued by a spontaneous joke.

Outdoors you'll find him in hardy clothes, munching edible weeds or tomatoes, parsley and walnuts from his clients' gardens. In winter he adds a tweed hat with ear flaps, otherwise it's a baseball cap from some nursery or his own olive green cap with the hemp leaf logo. He wore this once on a trip to Canada, where amongst other things, he did some weeding, and eating. Stopping to pick up a hitchhiker, he greeted him with a broad smile, revealing his teeth, stained blue by the dandelion roots he'd been eating. The hitchhiker took one look at him, another at the hemp logo, and immediately declined the lift. At Montreal airport the hat aroused some suspicion, and he was subjected to a body search. As soon as the sturdy old man began to undress in front of everyone, he was hastily waved through.

Oehme recently had a very different task to undertake. 'I'm being auctioned at the weekend,' he wrote to Germany. He was still a free man, it emerged, it was just a few hours of his valuable time that went under the hammer. It was a charity dinner and auction, and a personal consultation with the 'grass Pope' went to the highest bidder for a considerable sum. This is all part of his work, his routine.

Plans on sandwich wrappers
Wolfgang Oehme and his solo projects

It is dark outside and two figures move silently round Doris Lam's garden. Most people would have long since dialled 911. But Doris tries to make out if one of them is a stocky man, who stoops down every now and then. Yes; the man picking weeds and stroking the plants must be Wolfgang Oehme. In the mid-1970s, before he went into partnership with James van Sweden, Oehme was designing gardens in his neighbourhood. Sempeles, Dilatush, Schwartz, Freudenthal and Bear were some of the owners of these gardens, long since passed or moved away. We don't know what has become of these gardens. Others who put their gardens in Oehme's hands didn't realise that they would get to keep their designer, long after they had stopped paying him. 'Don't forget, they are all his gardens, and we are just the fortunate ones looking after them for him,' wrote Doris Lam. She

should have added that if the weeds grow too high, he appears in person to remove them. In his heart, land that he has made fruitful remains his. He has been at war with lawns ever since the 1960s. In his early years in the USA he couldn't replace these lawns with lavish plantings, lacking the variety to do so, instead he relied on pools, gravel and terraces made of cast concrete slabs, planted with individual perennials. This was all low-maintenance and didn't need feeding, mowing or watering. He first saw concrete slabs used on a visit to California, cast in redwood moulds, they were durable, easy to make and were very effective.

Left: With a very small choice of plants available to him in the US, Oehme's fight against the lawn in the early gardens of the mid-1960s was carried out mostly with stone, gravel and water.

Opposite: A more talented draughtsman would have made this look quite different. But this quick sketch on a sandwich wrapper was enough for the client, and the contractors, under Oehme's constant supervision, to create a fantastic garden (see pages 118/119).

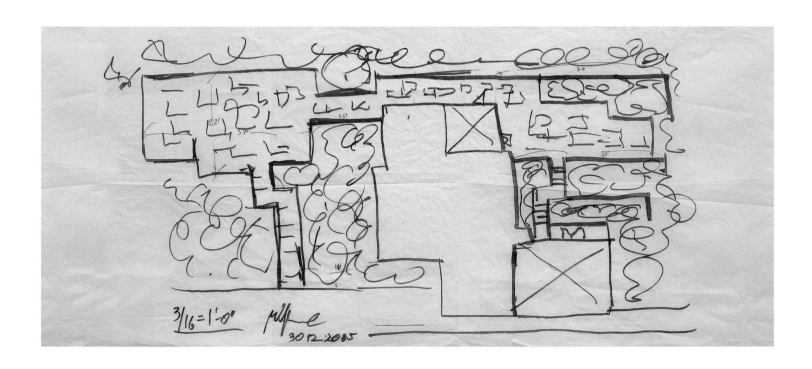

The garden of Mr and Mrs H.

Let us head to some of these solo projects in Baltimore County. Mr and Mrs H. still have their concrete slabs after well over twenty years, although some have been dislodged by the roots of a large maple tree. They retain much less heat than the darker Pennsylvania Bluestone, which later became Oehme's trademark paving stone. We have been invited for brunch at the home of Mr and Mrs H., and our hosts know exactly what to serve – they've known vegetarian Oehme for thirty years or more.

They collect art, and the view of the garden through a wall of glass takes in paintings, bowls and vases too. Their collection extends into the garden, dotted with sculptures by prominent artists like Barbara Hepworth, Karel Appel and John Henry. Lila Katzen from New York has also found a home here for one of her sculptures, alongside the work of less well known artists. A circular path guides us through this open air gallery, past the wide variety of weather proof art, a man made watercourse enlivens the scene, crowned by an old maple. In the

second half of the year *Miscanthus* hides the wire fence round the tennis court, planted on a small embankment that Oehme shaped from excavated soil. Amongst the riot of sculptural colour the *Oxydendron* stands out, with its extraordinary autumn foliage. Other than this, the plantings are muted and simple, a tranquil frame for the art. Even after several decades everything is still perfectly balanced. After brunch Mrs Marcia H. takes us for a tour. She has cut back her *Rudbeckia* 'Goldsturm' again, after they have faded, a quirk that Oehme describes as Marcia Syndrome. He disapproves of cutting back perennials in spring, but says nothing, preferring to look to the future or tell some of his old tales.

Wolfgang rolls out one of these old stories on our next drive, up into the hills. Even with his strong convictions, he keeps a sense of humour, as on one occasion when a client, who wanted a low maintenance garden, complained about a tree that would leave 'too much mess'. Oehme passed her a catalogue, saying here she would surely find some of her favourite trees. The client had to laugh at herself – it was a catalogue of plastic trees.

Garden of Mr and Mrs H.

Opposite: Created over twenty years ago, this is the second garden Oehme has designed for private art collectors Skeets and Marcia Harris. It has become an open air gallery for many of their sculptures.

Below left: With the midday autumn sun catching the *Miscanthus* fronds, the constantly changing plantlife complements the steel sculptures.

Below right: Skeets Harris and Wolfgang Oehme. Behind them the fence around the tennis court is masked by *Miscanthus*.

Garden of Mr and Mrs L.

Islands of high herbaceous perennials mark the way up to the main building of a large estate. A long driveway passes over a gently murmuring stream, heading gently uphill to the house and garden. Charles L. is a relaxed, perfectly groomed gentleman, who wants nothing to do with gardens, or perhaps just gardening. But when his garden was finished, he did make a comment that is always recalled whenever his name comes up: 'Wolfgang, this is fucking good.' He meant, of course, the wonderful combination of plants around the house and pool, the pool perfectly situated in front of the pale brown granite wall, which buffers the drop from the small plateau above, dotted with perennials. Irregular flagstones form a large terrace, into which the swimming pool is set, next to a more natural pond, surrounded by Oehme's signature plants. *Miscanthus giganteus*, *Solidago*, asters, *Pennisetum* and *Rudbeckia* 'Goldsturm'. The surrounding land can be seen from everywhere, resembling an English country park. The eye is caught by the occasional blemish here and there; any more would have spoiled the pure charm of the old landscape. Turkey vultures drift on the warm autumnal breeze, a buzzard can be heard, two German

Shepherds bark at their shadows, or at us – they don't seem to think much of their two-legged compatriots.

Garden of Mr and Mrs C.

Moving to the suburbs, we encounter a different aspect of the American landscape. The old trees are still there, sheltering the low houses, a last breath of the wild on the wind. The American homeowner feels secure in this tamed wilderness, armed with a droning lawnmower and clattering hedge trimmer. They plough on, over shadowed lawns that see the sun only now and then; the few evergreens take on forms that a psychologist might be able to explain. 'The poor things look like meatballs,' Oehme suggests.

The sun hangs low in the sky, framed by two solitary *Miscanthus* in Mr and Mrs C's garden, created by Oehme at the start of the 90s. Lorraine C. is more than happy with it. She has never found any reason to change anything about the structure, position or size of the pools, beds and open areas, although she has replaced the occasional plant that has run rampant. But it took a long time for her to impose her will. Years after its completion, she would still discover plants in her garden that had not been there the night before. Could he perhaps not be a little more modest with his gifts, she once asked him. Modesty won't make you famous, he replied with one of his huge grins. Nowadays he has found other things to keep him busy at night, but has been able to leave the garden in the tender care of its owner with a clear conscience. She is one of those clients who has developed a real sense of harmony with nature, and is able to fully engage with the garden. She had wanted a small water feature, but Oehme transformed this into a larger pool, a central element of the design, around which everything else revolved – flat surfaces, a space for the bench, a varied planting scheme with herbaceous perennials, grasses, roses and shrubs. A small sketch, done on the spot, was enough to explain it all to his client. Another clever design feature is the low wall which makes two gardens out of one. It separates the terrace near the living room from the larger area, which contains the pool. But you only notice this division in the garden – from the house it looks like one big area. At the end of the wall the path disappears behind some shrubs and under the trees becomes a wood chip path. It climbs a short but steep slope, and from a height of about 6 metres affords a measured view of the garden from above. Lorraine C. found a very apt and quite charming way to describe her designer: 'Has there ever been a man who carries, digs, plants and weeds with such vigour, and then gently rescues a bee from the swimming pool?' Oehme's love of animals is still with him.

Garden of Mr and Mrs L.
Opposite top left: Old maples provide shade for the front of the house. The granite path leads to the front door, and then across the lawn to the terrace and pool at the rear.

Opposite top right: A few steps lead up to the pool, which is set in a natural stone terrace. A matching wall elegantly holds back the sloping ground above.

Opposite below: Fountain grass surrounds an artificial pond below the house. Here Oehme has introduced a specifically horticultural aspect into an otherwise agricultural landscape.

Garden of Mr and Mrs C.
A circular path leads to the upper garden, from where almost all of the lower area can be seen. The small water feature originally intended has become an L-shaped pool.

Garden of Mr and Mrs C.

Top left: With a choice of plants quite new to this area, Oehme heightened the senses of his clients. The lady of the house in particular has become very involved in garden design.

Top right: The tall trees on the property provide the garden with shaded and half-shaded areas, which are brought to life by plants such as asters and astilbes.

Below left: Alongside his unusual grasses and perennials, Oehme now and then introduces exotic trees, such as *Acer griseum* from China.

Below right: The pool is crossed on two diagonal Pennsylvania Bluestone slabs, a versatile stone often used by Oehme in his gardens.

The garden is enclosed by a wooden fence that echoes
the landscape, fitting the natural garden and indeed
the whole wooded property perfectly.

The height difference between parking space and house was
skilfully overcome with stepped platforms. A cluster of
switchgrass adds a typical Oehme feel to the garden.

Garden of Mr and Mrs E.

It was far from certain that Mrs E. would be as happy
in her new house as she was in her previous one. Could
she really be content in this old house, in the shade of
the woods, having believed her dream home to be their
apartment designed by Mies van der Rohe? Her husband
wanted to move here, out of town, under giant maples,
oaks, beeches and evergreen magnolias, in a wooded
ravine. Mr and Mrs E. had no idea what sort of garden
could be created here, if any. Wolfgang Oehme used his
all purpose stone for paths and terraces, laid an impressive
Pennsylvania Bluestone staircase down the slope, and a
few steps lead from the front door down to an imposing
terrace. Oehme has tucked an L-shaped pool next to this
terrace, fed by a recycled waterfall that tumbles over large
rocks. This masks the rumble of traffic, audible even here.
The terrace runs right along the top of the slope, with
a railing only next to the house. A natural stone path
runs around to the back of the house. Around terrace
and pool grow *Leucanthemum superbum* 'Becky', *Inula
racemosa* 'Sonnenspeer', *Epimedium youngianum* 'Niveum'
and *Eupatorium cannabinum*. In the slightly thinned out
woods Oehme planted *Pycnanthemum muticum*, *Sambucus
ebulus* and *Petasites japonicus*. I asked how Wolfgang had
managed to make his ideas palatable to the lady of the
house. Her husband silently passed me Oehme's original
plan, a scribbled sketch, on an old sandwich wrapper. It
must have been something else, probably a gesture, his
generosity clad in a few words.

The garden in this shady wooded ravine is characterised by its generous dimensions. Pool, paths and terraces sit at right angles, here and there the plants will soon grow over the hard edges.

Going back to his roots
Journeys from his new to his old homeland

Top: Wolfgang Oehme found a new home in the USA more than fifty years ago, but is still in regular contact with friends and colleagues in Germany. The various newspapers and magazines for German Americans keep him up to date.

Below: Oehme (second from left) often visited his uncle Walter in Rothenburg, who in turn visited America until well into old age. From Rothenburg they would then drive to East Germany to visit friends and relatives.

For fifty years Wolfgang Oehme has travelled back and forth along the 40th parallel, give or take a few degrees. Even though the landscape and vegetation are not dissimilar, the population of the Baltimore area lives more in the sub-tropical south than in the temperate north. The lawnmowers are still busy at Christmas and by May most people have their air conditioning on non stop. Not Wolfgang – he doesn't worry too much about the weather. In extremis he'll go out weeding by moonlight, otherwise he just dresses appropriately and keeps active. 'With long sleeves you go kaputt,' he warns, and rolls up his own. Angst, realpolitik, kindergarten, blitzkrieg, schleppen, schnaps and lederhosen are now all part of the American vocabulary, just as kaputt is. Just a few reminders of the influence German immigrants have had. Whenever Wolfgang Oehme uses a German word, his voice becomes unusually clear, his intonation strong and positive. Is he really, in his heart, an American?

For fifty years, almost every year, Wolfgang has returned to Europe, mostly to Germany, his homeland. For him this means the places his family and friends, and his memories, live. The disappearance of his birthplace and the town where he grew up behind the Iron Curtain caused him much heartache, and trips to the former East Germany were complicated and difficult. He prefers to avoid such obstacles, but if he can't, then to overcome them quickly and painlessly. This was not possible during the Cold War. Even so, he managed to visit his parents,

friends and relatives half a dozen times, bringing coffee, chocolate and other luxury goods for them to share. They didn't know when he'd be back. But the lure of new seeds for the meagrely stocked nurseries in the US, was enough to draw him back. Wolfgang Oehme was one of those who firmly believed he had something to offer his new country, and that he could spread his ideas further and deeper than in provincial, middle class Germany. But the US was still a foreign country, culturally and linguistically, and Oehme still has Saxon blood in his veins. He often battled with homesickness on his long transatlantic flights. If not East Germany, he visited Hamburg, Frankfurt, Nürnberg or Berlin, all places with friends, and a history. Also on his itinerary was Rothenburg, where an uncle lived, or other beautiful places like Lake Constance or the Black Forest, and sometimes even Scandinavia. His son Roland came with him on many of these trips, even if it meant taking him out of school for a while. It's unlikely any American of his age has been to as many gardening shows and specialist nurseries as Roland Oehme. Whether he enjoyed it all is open to debate. But his father was always on the lookout for new things, and where better to satisfy his cravings than in the land of the garden show, in Zeppelin's Baden nursery or Hans Simon's in Marktheidenfeld, the demonstration garden in Weihenstephan or Hamburg's Planten un Blomen.

After reunification in 1990 Oehme concentrated his

visits on the new Federal states in the former East Germany. Just prior to this in 1989 Marianne Foerster wrote to him from Brussels: 'Dear Wolfgang, your package of plants arrived today, beautifully packed, still quite fresh! Can we send you one too? I'll keep some of it here, and take the rest to Bornim.' The need for secret seed packages ended soon after this, and the Berlin Wall came down. Potsdam-Bornim was accessible again and Oehme's drought was over. Almost simultaneously *Bold Romantic Gardens* by Oehme and van Sweden was published in Germany. Wolfgang gave several hundred copies to his old friend Dietmar Kummer in Chemnitz, who passed them on, not only to friends and relatives, but also to green space planning departments and contractors all over the country, spreading the word about Oehme and his work. In the following years the 'grass Pope', as the

Americans like to call him, always had his box of OvS slides to hand for the many lectures he gave. 'I'm not just the grass Pope, but the weed Pope too', he joked. One title is not enough for him.

Two weeks later he leaves his old home once again, and flies back to the new. Having returned from his 2006 trip to Germany with his son and Carol Oppenheimer, where they visited the Sansoucci Park in Potsdam, he reported excitedly that there were actual potatoes on Old Fritz's grave (Frederick the Great). That didn't mean much to his audience, but for him the potato is rooted in the German soil, sown by his own hands and vital for survival. He will always have his German hertiage. He'll return again next year, to Bitterfeld, Magdeburg, Chemnitz of course, everywhere he has left a trace, and that has left a trace in him.

Right: This picture from the 1970s shows Wolfgang on a visit to Freiberg in Saxony, between Chemnitz and Dresden.

Opposite: In 1988 Oehme visited Freising-Weihenstephan attending the ceremony to award the Karl Foerster Medal to Hermann Müssel. He also met the noted grass and perennials expert Ernst Pagels (with beret).

Full circle
Public projects in Magdeburg, Chemnitz and Bitterfeld

Left: Along with landscape architect Petra Pelz, Wolfgang transformed a monotonous lawn outside the Allianz building into this botanic jewel. This led to further collaborative projects.

Opposite left: The commission to design the gardens for the new town hall in Chemnitz was a great honour for Oehme. The low maintenance courtyard is in immaculate condition.

Opposite right: This block of flats in Chemnitz is enhanced by *Rudbeckia* 'Goldsturm', one of Oehme's trademarks, along with other robust, low maintenance grasses and perennials.

'Germany stands behind all that I do,' wrote the economist Friedrich List, when he was made a director of an American mining and railroad business. He had had to leave Germany in 1825, and achieved in America what had eluded him in Germany – respect and success. In a later diary entry, he summed up his experiences: 'Nothing elevates a man so much as the success of a large business.' He returned to Germany in 1832 and became the driving force behind the development of the German railway system. In contrast, Wolfgang Oehme was not forced into exile, but one thing does connect the two men, and many other creative, impatient emigrants – Germany won't let them go. If nothing else, it remains the place where they passed and failed their first exams, had their first disappointments and where success eluded them. America is a good place to plaster over these wounds, but true healing can only come about through acceptance in the land that once rejected you. One of Wolfgang Oehme's greatest pleasures is showing audiences in Chemnitz or Bitterfeld, Berlin or Magdeburg his work in America. Who would have expected the quiet, reticent loner to have become so successful? But he has. He is happy with his American lectures too, where he uses pictures of his work in Germany. He has shown

what he can do, and is recognised for it, even in 'good old Germany'. His slides show plantings of herbaceous perennials in front of the Allianz building in Magdeburg, newly planted courtyards and open spaces on a Chemnitz housing estate, a magnificent bed of grasses and perennials in redeveloped Bitterfeld. These are his gardens, made possible in America. It started in Magdeburg, where the landscape architect Petra Pelz designed the open spaces round the Allianz building in the suburb of Sudenburg in tandem with Oehme. His 1990 book had done the rounds here too, they decided they wanted to work with him, and a collaboration seemed the best option.

Before 1993, no-one dreamt that work on this scale was possible, but the city realised that even less experienced gardeners could achieve these results. And so a dreary lawn surrounded by tall trees became home to a plethora of herbaceous perennials, a bit of land of no interest to anyone turned into a precious pearl in the heart of town. Oehme had provided the inspiration, and the city wanted more. Whether in Magdeburg, Chemnitz or Bitterfeld, he would insist on handing out seedlings and rhizomes to other gardeners. *Aster oblongifolius* 'Dream of Beauty', *Fallopia japonica* 'Crimson beauty', *Pennisetum orientale* 'Tall Tails' and of course *Persicaria polymorpha* are just a few of the many robust plants that Oehme has filtered into the greenhouses of Germany's perennial specialists. Wolfgang has come full circle.

The Wolfsburg nurseryman Christian Baltin moved into top gear just after reunification, approaching the parks department in Magdeburg with his range of herbaceous perennials, thus establishing contact with Petra Pelz just as she was looking for this very thing. *Chrysanthemum pacificum*, *Senecio aureus*, *Panicum virgatum* 'Cloud Nine', all very successful in America, so why not in Germany? The fame of the Saxon from Maryland spread. Baltin was open to growing plants that Oehme preferred, and became the main source of plants for his German projects. It wasn't long before Oehme was invited to give a lecture in his birthplace, Chemnitz. Here too the so-called 'Oehme virus' took hold. And so Oehme and James van Sweden were able to get their hands on the courtyard of the new town hall, the Moritzhof. The arrival of the American stars on site certainly bemused the builders. They were used to seeing the local West German architect turn up for meetings in his best suit, but Wolfgang and Jim were more practically dressed, rolling up their sleeves and getting straight down to work. *Rudbeckia fulgida* 'Goldsturm' and *Sedum telephium* 'Herbstfreude' were soon planted around a multi-storey block in Promenadenstrasse too. He wouldn't have to translate it to 'Autumn Joy' around here. 'And now in Bitterfeld we also have a great sea of grasses and perennials growing next to the Goitzsche Lake,' rejoiced a Bitterfeld newspaper. In November 2000, Oehme wrote to a friend in Münster, 'here's the address of the head of the Department of Works in Bitterfeld, who's just been to visit me. He loved my garden, and took lots of plants with him. The circle is complete – from Bitterfeld to Washington and from Washington to Bitterfeld.' Every summer Oehme is to be found amongst the plants on the 2,500 square metre site next to the lake, liberating the plants from thistles and dandelions with a butter knife from his hotel. If you want to spend any time with him here, you'll need to tell an herbaceous perennial from a weed – and to have a strong back.

On his return from Germany in 1996, Oehme was chosen as 'Man of the Year' by the German Society of Maryland. Entering the hall for the award ceremony he proudly held up a shopping bag emblazoned with the name Chemnitz. The newspaper *Amerika Woche* had never seen such local patriotism before, and described his appearance as 'unique, quite non-conformist.' He would never hold up a bag from Baltimore in Chemnitz or Bitterfeld; that would be bragging.

Top left: Just as important as visiting friends on his annual trip to Bitterfeld, Oehme never fails to check on the state of the garden at the Bernstein villa.

Top right: Even though Wolfgang uses mostly low maintenance plants, weeding is inevitable. He and Carol Oppenheimer take care of that themselves.

Below right: The extravagance of this sea of flowers is one of the few glimmers of hope for Bitterfeld, still in decline after decades of pollution. A society for its long term preservation is to be formed.

Opposite left: Just a few years ago, all that lay between the Bernstein villa and the flooded brown coal pit Goitzsche was this patchy, bleak strip of grass.

Opposite right: To honour the contribution he has made to his second home town, this plaque was placed at one end of his wonderful garden of perennials.

Seduction of the masses
Petra Pelz: How Wolfgang Oehme changed my life as a landscape architect

Bold Romantic Gardens by James van Sweden and Wolfgang Oehme was the most inspirational book I read in the early 1990s, and from then on I was hooked. I saw the great fields of grasses, the sweeping spreads of the coneflower 'Goldsturm', opulent green bringing a powerful, calming and at the same time refreshing note to the hectic, often cursory pace of life amongst high buildings and wide roads and squares. I had never seen such dimensions and proportions before, and suddenly I was gripped by the urge to bring a distinctive, natural voice to such places, using luxuriant grasses and herbaceous perennials.

I had really very little experience with perennials, and a great many questions, so I wrote to Wolfgang Oehme. He phoned soon after, and a few weeks later was standing on my doorstep with an old school friend from Chemnitz. I couldn't quite believe it at first – he was offering to work with me. He really wanted to bring the work that had become his signature and trademark in America back to Germany. We were in luck – a project that had just started in the Halberstädter Strasse in Magdeburg was perfect for working on together. It had its problems, in that the plants, which were barely known here, were not available at all, or not in the quantities required. We only obtained enough *Persicaria polymorpha*, *Bistorta amplexicaule*, *Aralia cordata* and *Euphorbia palustris*, for example, with some difficulty. When we had got them all together, Oehme and James van Sweden arrived from America to lay out the plants

Opposite: Grasses and herbaceous perennials characterised Petra Pelz's creations at the International Garden Show in Rostock in 2003. Wolfgang and his son Roland (next to Petra) took the opportunity to meet her there.

Below: It was Wolfgang Oehme that inspired Petra Pelz to develop her use of herbaceous perennials in a way almost unknown at the time. Here is a section of her garden at the Rostock IGA with *Rudbeckia*, *Helenium* and *Calamagrostis*.

In Petra's own garden in Biederitz tall grasses and robust perennials
dominate, with some variation in the borders.

themselves. The landscape gardeners had never seen such a thing – architects flying in from the US and laying out the plants themselves! After that Wolfgang came to visit us in Magdeburg every year. He gave lectures, we went on trips to botanical gardens or visited nurseries. He rang me up almost every week, passing on invaluable tips and constantly expanding my knowledge. *Persicaria polymorpha Tanacetum macrophyllum*, or *Euphorbia palustris* are just a few of the hardy plants that Wolfgang brought to my attention.

The virus had got me. I went on journeys, to meetings of the international group Perennial Perspectives, travelled round Europe with co-members, learned about other styles of planting and plenty of new plants. These experiences helped me to flesh out Oehme's large scale style and adapt it to our own circumstances.

The main difference between the USA and our situation is that most gardens here are significantly smaller. But to think that Oehme and van Sweden's principles have no relevance for smaller gardens would be wrong – spaciousness, tranquillity and clarity are criteria that are just as important for our gardens. Certainly, proportions must be altered to suit the dimensions, but keeping the focus on robust plants, an ever changing *mise en scène*, and large groupings of plants are all aspects that can enrich gardens here too.

The large scale use of grasses and herbaceous perennials in public green spaces is often criticised as boring and very unsatisfying, especially if specific varieties don't work. Every design style has its advantages and disadvantages, but in my opinion the former are becoming ever more apparent. With sturdy plants that are suited to their urban environments, the care and management of these spaces is much simplified. The conditions for an integrated, long lived and low maintenance planting are created with groupings of plants that have similar needs and that regenerate themselves well.

Wolfgang Oehme has spent decades doggedly searching out valuable plants, and continues to do so, with much buried treasure still to be found in the botanical gardens. This is what makes our work so exciting; within the 'Oehme concept' there are endless possible variations of large-scale plantings. Oehme, now nearing eighty and as hungry as ever for new knowledge, leaves no stone unturned in passing on his expertise.

Petra Pelz is a landscape architect in Magdeburg. An expert in herbaceous perennials, her own style of design has developed from her long friendship with Wolfgang Oehme.

Building a legacy
A final assesment of Oehme's work

Left: Without his work over several decades, these grasses would not have been seen in front of Towson's shopping mall, claims Oehme, not without some justification.

Opposite: Wolfgang is a firm believer in natural processes. Tall *Miscanthus* grow out of carpets of *Rudbeckia fulgida* 'Goldsturm' (left) or *Physostegia virginiana* (right). Every year the smaller plants have to fight off others to maintain their territory.

How different would the world be today if his car had kept on going and he had never stopped by the roadside? It's hard to say. No-one can know how many seeds collected by Wolfgang Oehme next to the autobahn in the 1970s have taken root in the USA, and since been included in nurserymen's catalogues. Often enough, he would order drivers to pull over, so he could fill his little bags with plants or seeds. He would always return with some of these lightweight souvenirs. His house in Towson is still littered with drying seeds and pips collected in his neighbourhood, near Chesapeake Bay or in the Appalachians, to be given life again somewhere else in the US. Seven decades after his first steps in the gardening world, Oehme is still entranced by the constant renewal of the plant world. 'Old age is no protection from youthful passion', said Karl Foerster, and he was right again.

Youthful passion still drives Oehme on, by car along America's highways and byways. His face darkens when he sees a 'mow and blow company' of untrained workers crashing round the suburbs with lawnmowers and leafblowers. He would have loved to get rid of them. But his mood lifts and he chats excitedly when he discovers a clump of *Miscanthus* in front of the shopping centre, grasses and robust perennials on a roundabout, the non-invasive fleece flower *Persicaria polymorpha* or

another of his favourites in a front garden. Thirty years ago none of that was here. His seed has grown, people have begun to understand. It has not all been in vain. While Oehme continues to conquer public and private land metre by metre with his tireless commitment to grasses and herbaceous perennials, his place amongst the most important contemporary gardeners has long since been assured. His name crops up in almost every book on the use of plants, and no conference on herbaceous perennials and grasses takes place without Oehme or van Sweden being mentioned. Their first book together, *Bold Romantic Gardens* is now out of print, the few available copies selling for hundreds of dollars on the internet,

and the German edition, also out of print, barely to be found at all. Oehme and van Sweden have thrown open the windows, brought light to the darker corners of the gardening world, and a new perspective to those who have never given themselves heart and soul to either the native gardening movement or the classical school of design. Fresh air has swept through academia, the media and bookshops. Another way has been found, somewhere between the insistence on native plants and the design idea of a 'threesome in complimentary colours with 10 percent white'. There have certainly been large plantings of just one variety before, but this has never been laid down as a principle.

If the concept of Romanticism springs easily to mind, Oehme and van Sweden have never overdone this. If they are trying to achieve any particular effect, it is one of relaxed spaciousness. Things exist as they are in their gardens. The effect connects two sides, which both influence us and conflict within us – nature and culture, informality and order. Like the robust plants Oehme loves, and despite all our efforts at domestication, we remain part of nature and can never entirely escape it. Indeed some of us want to return to it. The large groupings, studded with towering solitary specimens merge to create grand, highly artistic pictures, art in rhythm with the seasons. We're not hunter-gatherers anymore, not fools but cultivated people. We want to surround ourselves with art – as long as it doesn't involve too much work. And that is the charm of Oehme's system. If you follow his instructions precisely, both large and small gardens are easy enough to look after. Without any sort of care the assertiveness of wild plants and weeds will of course triumph over most gardens, but then culture won't function without some sort of care, never mind horticulture. 'Keep it simple' is thus the best advice, but even the simplest garden takes a great deal of planning. Just which plants suit which soil and light conditions and are best for fore- or background planting can only be mastered with years of experience and an educated imagination. Oehme and van Sweden are often copied, in America, Asia, Europe, and they are happy if it works. What more could they ask? But they are angry if it does not; the client deserves better than that.

Many plants have reached a wider use because of their arrangement in massive groups, only attracting the attention of the amateur gardener because of such striking features. Most are undemanding and grow easily into thickets, but others do tend to run rampant. Oehme puts such plants next to each other, holding each other in check. The first signs of climate change have resulted in some interesting developments, like the early flowering *Miscanthus*, which have started to self-seed in the sandy, mild coastal areas. For Oehme, nothing could be better for spreading the reach of his plants. As he has aged, so has his liking for plants that run wild. With every *Petasites*, every *Macleaya*, Oehme runs wild too. 'When I'm gone, my plants will continue to grow and grow and grow and grow.' An exciting prospect for any gardener.

And so the last word falls to Karl Foerster, who showed our hero the way and so often managed to express exactly how Oehme feels. 'If I ever return to earth, I'll be a gardener again. And the time after that. This job is too big for just one life.' Wolfgang Oehme, and all seed-collecting, inquisitive, energetic gardeners and garden designers will feel totally at home with this sentiment.

Above: Oehme draws the strength and energy needed for such an active gardening life from his unshakeable optimism and the firm belief that he is doing the right thing. This picture shows him in a recently completed garden near his home.

Opposite: Amongst the most important virtues of a good garden designer is restraint, Oehme believes. The choice in the nurseries has increased enormously, and dissipation of effect is an ever present danger. Less is sometimes more.

Wolfi-plants
Wolfgang Oehme's favourite plants

For years Wolfgang Oehme was associated above all with mass plantings of *Rudbeckia* 'Goldsturm', *Sedum* 'Autumn Joy' and *Pennisetum*. But the inquisitive Oehme is always looking for new plants, and so has added many other trademark plants to his repertoire over the years. His constant, stubborn promotion of the non-invasive *Persicaria polymorpha* has become famous, almost infamous. He manages to sing its praises in every conversation he has with gardeners, nurserymen, university professors or garden designers. Four qualities – stability, robustness, flowering duration and competitiveness – make *Persicaria polymorpha* the benchmark for all so-called Wolfi-plants. This is the term used by his staff for the large collection of herbaceous perennials, grasses and trees that Wolfgang

Oehme has come to value over the years and to which he always confidently returns. Not all of this list is currently available in Europe – all the more reason to name them and investigate their use in our corner of the world.

For the purposes of this book, editor and author had to make a decision: should we show fifteen plants with pictures and information, or 160, a comprehensive list for which the curious reader can seek out their own information from other sources? We have opted for the latter, together with a considerable selection of images.

Carex muskingumensis 'Oehme'   *Solidago rugosa* 'Fireworks'   *Asteromoea mongolica*

Rudbeckia maxima   *Rhus chinensis* 'September Beauty'   *Pennisetum orientale* 'Tall Tails'

Herbaceous Perennials

Acanthus hungaricus – Hungarian bear's breeches
Agastache 'Blue Fortune' – anise hyssop
Alchemilla mollis – lady's mantle
Amsonia hubrichtii – thread-leaf blue star
Aralia cordata – Japanese spikenard
Aster macrophyllus 'Albus' – large leaf aster
Aster macrophyllus 'Twilight' – large leaf aster
Aster oblongifolius 'October Skies' – aromatic aster
Aster oblongifolius 'Raydon's Favourite' – aromatic aster
Aster tataricus – Tatarian aster
Asteromoea mongolica – double Japanese aster
Bistorta amplexicaulis 'Firetail' – red flowering knotweed
Brunnera macrophylla – Siberian bugloss

Calamintha nepeta subsp. nepeta – dwarf calamint
Centaurea jacea – knapweed
Datisca cannabina – false hemp
Eupatorium cannabinum – hemp agrimony
Eupatorium hyssopifolium – hyssopleaf thoroughwort
Eupatorium maculatum 'Riesenschirm' – Joe Pye weed
Euphorbia palustris – spurge
Fallopia japonica 'Crimson Beauty' – crimson clump forming knotweed
Gaura lindheimeri 'Whirling Butterflies' – butterfly gaura
Geranium macrorrhizum – cranesbill
Geranium 'Rozanne' – hardy geranium 'Rozanne'
Gillenia trifoliata – bowman's root
Helenium 'Flammenspiel' – sneezeweed

Datisca cannabina

Sedum telephium 'Herbstfreude'

Eupatorium hyssopifolium

Persicaria polymorpha

Pennisetum alopecuroides

Aesculus parviflora

Helianthus angustifolius 'Gold Lace' – swamp sunflower

Helleborus orientalis – Lenten rose

Heuchera villosa 'Autumn Bride' – hairy alumroot 'Autumn Bride'

Hibiscus moscheutos 'Lady Baltimore' – swamp rose mallow

Hosta 'Sum and Substance'

Inula racemosa 'Sonnenspeer' – elecampane

Ligularia dentata 'Desdemona'

Liriope muscari 'Big Blue' – liriope 'Big Blue'

Lysimachia clethroides – gooseneck loosestrife

Macleaya cordata – plume poppy

Malva alcea var. *fastigiata* – hollyhock mallow

Nepeta x *faassenii* – blue catmint

Origanum 'Rosenkuppel' – 'Rosenkuppel' oregano

Perovskia atriplicifolia – Russian sage

Persicaria polymorpha – giant Himalayan fleece flower

Petasites japonicus – bog rhubarb or giant butterbur

Physostegia virginiana – obedient plant

Pycnanthemum muticum – short-toothed mountain mint

Rohdea japonica – Chinese sacred lily

Rudbeckia fulgida 'Goldsturm' – black eyed Susan

Rudbeckia nitida 'Herbstsonne' – Autumn sun black eyed Susan

Rudbeckia subtomentosa – sweet black eyed Susan

Sambucus ebulus – herbaceous dwarf elder

Sedum 'Herbstfreude' – Autumn joy

Sedum makinoi 'Matrona' – stonecrop hybrid 'Matrona'

Senecio aureus – ragwort or golden groundsel

Solidago rugosa 'Fireworks' – goldenrod

Stachys byzantina 'Countess Helen von Stein' – large leaf lamb's ear

Trachystemon orientalis – Oriental borage

Valeriana officinalis – valerian

Veronicastrum sibiricum – Culver's root

Yucca filamentosa – Adam's needle

Grasses

Acorus gramineus 'Ogon' – grassleaf sweet flag or Japanese rush

Calamagrostis x *acutiflora* 'Karl Foerster' – feather reed grass

Helianthus angustifolius 'Gold Lace'

Aster oblongifolius 'October Skies'

Hibiscus moscheutos 'Lady Baltimore'

Fallopia japonica 'Crimson Beauty'

Rosa 'Knock Out'

Geranium 'Rozanne'

Carex elata – tufted sedge
Carex morrowii 'Ice Dance' – Japanese sedge
Carex muskingumensis 'Oehme' – palm sedge 'Oehme'
Carex pendula – great drooping sedge
Hakonechloa macra – hakone grass
Miscanthus x *giganteus* – giant miscanthus
Miscanthus 'Purpurascens' – flame grass
Miscanthus sinensis 'Adagio' – Japanese silver grass
Miscanthus sinensis 'Malepartus' – 'Malepartus' Japanese
silver grass
Molinia caerulea subsp. *arundinacea* 'Windspiel' – tall
purple moor grass
Panicum amarum 'Dewey Blue' – bitter panic grass
Panicum virgatum 'Cloud Nine' – switch grass 'Cloud Nine'
Panicum virgatum 'Northwind' – switch grass 'Northwind'
Panicum virgatum 'Rotstrahlbusch' – switch grass
'Rotstrahlbusch'
Pennisetum alopecuroides – fountain grass
Pennisetum compressum 'Moudry' – black fountain grass
Pennisetum orientale 'Tall Tails' – Oriental pennisetum
'Tall Tails'

Spodiopogon sibiricus – frost grass or silver spikegrass

Ferns
Dryopteris x *australis* – dixie wood fern
Dryopteris erythrosora – Autumn fern
Matteuccia struthiopteris – ostrich fern
Polystichum polyblepharum – Japanese tassle fern

Swamp and water plants
Acorus calamus – common sweet flag
Ceratophyllum demersum – hornwort
Iris pseudacorus – yellow flag iris
Nelumbo lutea – American Lotus or Yellow Lotus
Nelumbo nucifera – Indian lotus, sacred lotus
or bean of India
Nuphar japonica – Japanese pond lily
or dwarf spatterdock lily
Nymphaea – water lily
Orontium aquaticum – golden club
Pontederia cordata – pickerel weed
Sagittaria latifolia – broadleaf arrowhead

Polystichum polyblepharum   *Hydrangea paniculata* 'Tardiva'   *Ligularia dentata* 'Desdemona'

Aster tataricus   *Matteucia struthiopteris*   *Rudbeckia subtomentosa*

Saururus cernuus – lizard's tail
Scirpus sylvaticus – wood club rush
Thalia dealbata – thalia or powdery alligator-flag
Typha minima – dwarf bulrush or dwarf reedmace

Climbers
Aristolochia macrophylla (or *A. durior*) – common
Dutchman's pipe
Bignonia capreolata – crossvine
Decumaria barbara 'Barbara Ann' – wood vamp
Hydrangea petiolaris – climbing hydrangea
Lonicera sempervirens – trumpet honeysuckle
Schizophragma hydrangeoides 'Moonlight' – Japanese
hydrangea vine
Vitis coignetiae – crimson glory vine

Bamboos
Bambusa multiplex 'Alphonso-Karrii' – hedge bamboo
'Alphonse Karr'
Fargesia murielae – umbrella bamboo
Fargesia nitida – great wall bamboo
Fargesia robusta – clumping bamboo
Fargesia rufa – fountain Bamboo

Phyllostachys aureosulcata f. *aureocaulis* – golden
crookstem bamboo or golden groove bamboo

Trees
Alnus glutinosa – black alder or common alder
Celtis occidentalis 'Magnifica' – hackberry or sugar
hackberry
Clerodendrum trichotomum var. *fargesii* – harlequin
glorybower
Cornus kousa – Chinese dogwood
Ilex 'Nellie R. Stevens' – 'Nellie R. Stevens' holly
Magnolia grandiflora 'Bracken's Brown Beauty' –
'Bracken's Brown Beauty' southern magnolia
Magnolia virginiana – sweetbay magnolia
Nyssa sylvatica – black tupelo
Pinus bungeana – lacebark pine
Pinus flexilis 'Vanderwolf's Pyramid' – 'Vanderwolf's
Pyramid' or limber pine
Pterocarya fraxinifolia – caucasian wing nut
Rhus chinensis 'September Beauty' – Chinese sumac
Styrax japonicus – Japanese snowbell
Syringa reticulata – Japanese tree lilac
Tamarix ramosissima – saltcedar

Lysimachia clethroides

Miscanthus sinensis 'Purpurascens'

Sedum maximum 'Matrona'

Physostegia virginiana 'Vivid'

Haconechloa macra

Micanthus sinensis 'Malepartus'

Shrubs

Aesculus parviflora – bottlebrush buckeye
Amelanchier canadensis – Juneberry or snowy mespilus
Aronia arbutifolia 'Brilliantissima' – red chokeberry
Chionanthus retusus – Chinese fringe tree
Cornus mas – cornelian cherry
Corylopsis pauciflora – Winter hazel
Edgeworthia papyrifera – Oriental paperbush
Elaeagnus x ebbingei – elaeagnus or Ebbing's silverberry
Hamamelis x intermedia 'Arnold Promise' – witch hazel
Heptacodium miconioides – seven-son flower
Hydrangea paniculata 'Tardiva' – panicle hydrangea
Ilex verticillata – American Winterberry
or common winterberry
Indigofera heterantha – Himalayan indigo
Mahonia bealei – leatherleaf mahonia
Mahonia x media 'Winter Sun' – mahonia hybrid
Myrica cerifera – wax myrtle
Nandina domestica – heavenly bamboo
Osmanthus fragrans – sweet osmanthus or sweet olive
Photinia davidiana var. *undulata* – Chinese stranvaesia
Photinia davidiana var. *undulata* 'Prostrata' –
Chinese photinia

Photinia davidiana 'Winterthur'
Rosa 'Knock Out' – 'Knock Out' rose
Rosa rugosa – rugosa rose or Japanese rose
Rubus odoratus – purple-flowering raspberry
Rubus parviflorus – thimbleberry
Salix elaeagnos – hoary willow
Sarcococca hookeriana var. *humilis* – Christmas box
or sweet box
Sorbaria sorbifolia – Ural false spiraea
Spiraea latifolia – broadleaf meadowsweet
or white meadowsweet
Tetrapanax papyrifer – rice paper tree
Viburnum x burkwoodii 'Conoy' – 'Conoy' burkwood
viburnum
Viburnum carlesii – Korean spice viburnum
Viburnum dilatatum – linden viburnum
Viburnum 'Pragense' – Prague viburnum
Viburnum prunifolium – blackhaw viburnum
Viburnum setigerum – tea viburnum
Viburnum sieboldii – Siebold's viburnum

Fargesia murielae

Perovskia atriplicifolia

Acanthus hungaricus

Pennisetum compressum 'Moudry'

Pycnanthemum muticum

Miscanthus sinensis 'Malepartus'

Appendix
Credits and acknowledgements

Picture credits

All pictures not referred to here are the author's own.

The author is grateful for the following pictures:

Lennart Constant: page 127 right
Sidney Emmer: page 109, sketch by Oehme
Richard Felber: page 43
Roger Foley: page 62
Roland Oehme: page 96 bottom
Wolfgang Oehme archive: pages 6 top, 7, 10, 11, 12 (2), 15 top, 17, 19, 22 (2), 23, 24 (2), 25 (2), 38 (2), 41, 46, 64, 80, 86 top, 87 plan by Ching-Fang Chen, 88, 95, 98, 99, 100, 103, 108, 120 bottom, 122, 123, 124, 125 right, 126 left, 128 bottom, 134, 136 bottom (3), 137 top centre and right, bottom left and right, 139 top right, 140 top left and right, bottom left and centre, 141 top left and right.
Office of Oehme van Sweden Ass.: pages 28, 45, 66 top, 92 (2), 93
Carol Oppenheimer: page 125 left, front flap
Petra Pelz: pages 128 top, 129, 130
Inge Richter: pages 15 bottom, 16
Gary Rogers: page 21
Imma Schmidt: page 131
James van Sweden: pages 36, 65
Ulrich Zielke: page 18

Bibliography

Rudolf Borchardt: *Der leidenschaftliche Gärtner*, Stuttgart 1968
Naomi Brooks (ed): *Collection of essays celebrating Wolfgang Oehme's 75th birthday*, 2005
Karel Čapek: *Das Jahr des Gärtners*, München 1970
Karl Foerster: *Warnung und Ermutigung*, Berlin 1974
Karl Foerster: *Der Einzug der Farne und Gräser in unsere Gärten*, Radebeul 1978
Karl Foerster: *Der Steingarten der sieben Jahreszeiten*, Leipzig/ Radebeul 1981
Karl Foerster: *Ein Garten der Erinnerung*, Berlin 1982
Roger Grounds: *Gräser*, München 2007
Wolfgang Koeppen: *Amerikafahrt*, Stuttgart 1959
Köhlein, Menzel, Bärtels: *Das große Ulmer-Buch der Gartenpflanzen*, Stuttgart 2000
Wolfgang Oehme, James van Sweden: *Die Neuen Romantischen Gärten*, München 1990
Heinz Ohff: *Der grüne Fürst*, München 1993
Ludwig Heinrich Hermann Graf von Pückler-Muskau: *Andeutungen über Landschaftsgärtnerei*, Frankfurt am Main 1996
James van Sweden: *Gardening with Water*, New York 1995
James van Sweden: *Gardening with Nature*, New York 1997

Acknowledgements

My thanks go first of all to Wolfgang Oehme. A book like this can only succeed with a great deal of commitment, seriousness and mutual confidence, but also with a good pinch of humour. In the USA, Carol Oppenheimer was exceptionally helpful, and deserves my praise: without Wolfgang Oehme's constant companion the difficulties would have been much greater. Likewise Roland Oehme, who passed on a great deal of information and provided an indispensable email link between Baltimore and Münster. At the office of Oehme and van Sweden, Steel Colony, Christine Kelly and Ching-Fang Chen were always available with information and photographs, and made contact with James van Sweden much easier. For their hospitality I must thank in particular Carole and Alex Rosenberg, and Kurt Bluemel, but also all those whose gardens I was permitted to visit and photograph. Many of Wolfgang Oehme's friends and acquaintances in the USA and Germany have spent a good deal of time answering my questions. I am grateful to Roland Thomas at DVA for his constant support of this project and for his delicate touch. Susanne Ebersberger has created another lovely book from my words and pictures. And finally thanks to Julian Richter of Richter Play Equipment (unitedplay.com) in Frasdorf for sponsoring this project.

Frances Lincoln Ltd
4 Torriano Mews
Torriano Avenue
London NW5 2RZ
www.franceslincoln.com

ISBN 978-0-7112-2750-7

Printed and bound in Singapore